# The Alienated Librarian

**Recent Titles in
New Directions in Information Management**

Financing Information Services: Problems, Changing Approaches, and New Opportunities for Academic and Research Libraries
*Peter Spyers-Duran and Thomas W. Mann, Jr., editors*

Issues in Academic Librarianship: Views and Case Studies for the 1980s and 1990s
*Peter Spyers-Duran and Thomas W. Mann, Jr., editors*

Information Specialist as Team Player in the Research Process
*Julie M. Neway*

The Politics of Public Librarianship
*David Shavit*

Subject Access to Visual Arts Resources Collections: A Model for Computer Construction of Thematic Catalogs
*Karen Markey*

Unions for Academic Library Support Staff: Impact on Workers and the Workplace
*James M. Kusack*

Circulation Policy in Academic, Public, and School Libraries
*Sheila S. Intner*

Management Theory and Library Education
*Sajjad ur Rehman*

Libraries in Prisons: A Blending of Institutions
*William J. Coyle*

The Academic Library Director: Management Activities and Effectiveness
*Joanne R. Euster*

The New Path: Undergraduate Libraries at United States and Canadian Universities, 1949–1987
*Roland Conrad Person*

Local Area Networks in Information Management
*Harry M. Kibirige*

Recruiting, Educating, and Training Cataloging Librarians: Solving the Problems
*Sheila S. Intner and Janet Swan Hill, editors*

Z
682.35
P82
N38
1989

# The Alienated Librarian

Marcia J. Nauratil

NEW DIRECTIONS IN INFORMATION
MANAGEMENT, NUMBER 20

Greenwood Press
New York • Westport, Connecticut • London

AUDREY COHEN COLLEGE LIBRARY
75 Varick St. 12th Floor
New York, NY 10013

**Library of Congress Cataloging-in-Publication Data**

Nauratil, Marcia J.
  The alienated librarian.
  (New directions in information management,
0887-3844 ; no. 20)
  Bibliography: p.
  Includes index.
  1. Librarians—Psychology.  2. Library science—
Psychological aspects.  3. Alienation (Social psychology)
4. Burnout (Psychology)  I. Title.  II. Series.
Z682.35.P82N38  1989      020'.019        88-34797
ISBN 0-313-25996-8 (lib. bdg. : alk. paper)

British Library Cataloguing in Publication Data is available.

Copyright © 1989 by Karl A. Nauratil, Jr.

All rights reserved. No portion of this book may be
reproduced, by any process or technique, without the
express written consent of the publisher.

Library of Congress Catalog Card Number: 88-34797
ISBN: 0-313-25996-8
ISSN: 0887-3844

First published in 1989

Greenwood Press, Inc.
88 Post Road West, Westport, Connecticut   06881

Printed in the United States of America

The paper used in the book complies with the
Permanent Paper Standard issued by the National
Information Standards Organization (Z39.48-1984).

10 9 8 7 6 5 4 3 2

**Copyright Acknowledgment**

The author gratefully acknowledges permission to quote from
"Refuse to be Burnt-Out" by The Fugs, © New Rose Records, 1985.

For Larry, my parents,
and Karl

# Contents

| | |
|---|---|
| *Preface* | ix |
| 1. The Burnout Phenomenon | 1 |
| 2. Work, Alienation, and the Human Service Professions | 11 |
| 3. Librarianship: An Inevitable Case? | 37 |
| 4. Fuel for Burnout: Current Trends | 63 |
| 5. Coping and Beyond | 83 |
| *Selected Bibliography* | 111 |
| *Index* | 125 |

# Preface

A surprisingly large number of librarians do not feel fulfilled in their work, but frustrated, stressed, and oppressed. This book will examine both the various factors involved in the development of this unhappy state of affairs and also the corresponding variety of solutions available to those concerned with its amelioration. I will argue that to understand and substantially reduce the rapidly growing incidence of burnout among librarians, we must look beyond the individual victim to the structural organization of the labor process in which he or she participates and, above all, to the distribution of decision-making power in the workplace.

Professional work, especially a career in the human service professions, has long been esteemed as a singularly appropriate way to contribute to the betterment of the lot of humankind. The worthiness of such occupations is expressed in the strength of their designation as "vocations" to which one is "called"; etymologically, professionals can trace their own special status back to that of the men and women of the medieval church, whose "profession of faith" marked their acceptance of holy orders. The honorific aura of professionalism continues to suggest the dedication of the highest human abilities to a sacred calling of general social benefit. Remote as its resemblance to the mundane realities of professional practice may well be in any given instance, such imagery still figures prominently as a source of motivation and serves very well as a recruitment device. Librarians, along with their sister professionals in education, nursing, and social work, for whom the purely economic rewards of a professional career are generally rather less than those for physicians or lawyers, appear to take such ideals relatively seriously.

Why, then, we must ask, do so many professional librarians come to relate to their work as essentially "just another job"—a reasonably clean means to a paycheck, but also too often both a source of insupportable stress and a pointless treadmill trek to nowhere? Why do librarians, of all people, burn out?

My search for answers to these questions has taken me a bit beyond the boundaries of library science proper but not, I believe, very far from the practical experience of working librarians. I am grateful to the many librarians who took the time to share with me their thoughts and feelings on the issues raised in this book, particularly the late Dick Gervickas of the Rochester, New York, Public Library system. I am also grateful for the insights and encouragement offered freely by Dr. Margaret Anderson, the late Dr. Laurent-G. Denis, and other friends and colleagues at the Faculty of Library and Information Science of the University of Toronto, my friends and colleagues in Montreal, and those I met at the 1986 Tri-State Conference in Topeka, Kansas. Thanks are due to the library staff at the Washington Irving Center in Madrid for their assistance in obtaining the materials that allowed me to begin my research for this book while in Spain, and to my brother- and sister-in-law, Ed and Denise Nauratil, whose informal conversations with me on parallel problems in medical work encouraged me to broaden the scope of my inquiry. Finally, for his willingness to listen, think, and talk past dawn, many thanks to my husband, sociologist Karl A. Nauratil, Jr.

# The Alienated Librarian

# 1

# The Burnout Phenomenon

> My life is bitter as wormwood; the very life is burning out of me. I'm a poor, miserable, forlorn drudge. . . . What's the use of our trying to do anything, trying to know anything, trying to be anything? What's the use of living? I wish I was dead!
>
> Harriet Beecher Stowe, *Uncle Tom's Cabin*

Echoes of this lament by the ill-treated slave George Harris can be heard daily at the reference desk, at the video display terminal, and in the administrative offices of many libraries. To people outside the profession, this problem often comes as a surprise. Librarianship is popularly viewed as a pleasant and non-stressful sinecure in a quiet booklined setting, with relaxing routines gently punctuated by towheaded tots arriving for story hour and by chats with gray-haired matrons searching for fresh mysteries. This persistent image of librarians and information professionals has found its way into the literature of occupational stress. In a recent British study, 150 occupations were rated on a "stress scale" of one to ten. Miners were considered the most stressed at 8.3, police were rated 7.7, bus drivers 4.8, beauticians 3.5, museum workers 2.8, and librarians the lowest at 2.2. When these results were published in the American press, librarians responded with outrage, many writing letters to the editors of their local newspapers to protest the low rating. A San Francisco librarian argued that the stress rating should be similar to that of bus drivers, as "we attract the same kind of people the Muni drivers get in fights with."[1]

## BURNOUT: WHAT IS IT?

While burnout has been the subject of social scientific analysis only since the mid-1970s, connotations for the term extend back at least two and a half centuries. Many of these evoke vivid images. A 1710 definition of burnout refers to the forcible expulsion from one's home because of fire.[2] George Harris' cry that "the very life is burning out of me" represents an early application of the term to a process occurring within the individual. The disillusion and despair of Querry in Graham Greene's 1961 novel, *A Burnt-Out Case*, provide an ominous prototype for today's burnt-out professionals. Later in the decade, burnout came to describe the mental and emotional damage caused by excessive use of psychoactive drugs.

Psychiatrist Herbert Freudenberger is generally credited with first using the term burnout to denote physical and emotional responses to work-related stress. Using a case-study approach that emphasizes individual psychology, Freudenberger defines burnout as a "state of fatigue or frustration brought about by devotion to a cause, way of life, or relationship that failed to produce the expected reward."[3] Other researchers focus on burnout as a process rather than an end state, viewing it as a "progressive loss of idealism, energy, and purpose experienced by people in the helping professions as a result of the conditions of their work."[4] Psychologist Cary Cherniss defines burnout somewhat more broadly as "a process in which the professional's attitudes and behavior change in negative ways in response to job strain."[5] Researchers Pines and Aronson subsume burnout under the rubric of tedium. Both states, they maintain, "are characterized by physical depletion, by feelings of helplessness and hopelessness, by emotional drain, and by the development of negative attitudes toward work, life, and other people." While they view tedium as resulting from any prolonged chronic pressure—mental, physical, or emotional—they consider burnout to be the result of "constant or repeated *emotional pressure* associated with an intense involvement with *people* over long periods of time."[6]

Pioneer researcher Christina Maslach also addresses burnout as a syndrome affecting individuals engaged in "people work" of some kind.[7] She has analyzed the many definitions of the phenomenon and found agreement on three key dimensions. The first is exhaustion. While this is sometimes physical, the burnt-out individual is more often psychologically or emotionally exhausted. He or she is typically described as being worn-out, without energy, depleted. Burnt-out individuals experience a loss of feeling, a loss of interest and concern, even a loss of spirit. The second key dimension of the burnout syndrome is a negative shift in the way the individual responds or relates to other people, especially to clients. There is generally a movement toward depersonalization; the burnt-out worker often experiences loss of idealism and develops negative or inappropriate attitudes toward the very people he or she set out to serve. The third dimension is a negative response to oneself and one's personal accomplishments. This is variously described as depression, low morale, withdrawal, and inability to cope.[8]

## THE EFFECTS OF BURNOUT

Burnout can have profound negative consequences for individual librarians, for the library, and for users. On the individual level, health often deteriorates. The relationship between occupational stress and such health problems as coronary disease and ulcers has been recognized for decades. Emotional exhaustion often accompanies physical exhaustion. Sleep disturbances may occur. Susceptibility to viruses and infections increases with chronic fatigue. Other physiological responses to burnout include headaches, frequent and prolonged colds, muscular pain, gastrointestinal disorders, increased premenstrual tension, and amenorrhea. Burnout can also provoke flare-ups of such preexisting medical conditions as asthma, diabetes, and high blood pressure.[9] People experiencing burnout may engage in coping behaviors—overeating, smoking, alcohol or drug abuse—that in turn create further physical, emotional, and performance problems.

Burnout poses a serious threat to individuals' psychological well-being. The reduced sense of personal accomplishment that is a central element of the burnout syndrome can become a generalized loss of self-esteem, affecting not only one's work life but one's personal life as well. A variety of emotional symptoms may appear, ranging from irratability and inability to concentrate to depression and paranoia. Relationships with colleagues, clients, friends, and family members may suffer. Burnt-out librarians are likely to experience negative changes in their attitudes, becoming cynical about their work and hostile toward the library and its constituency: more than one librarian has referred to his or her branch as "the zoo." They may come to feel that their professional activities—or even their lives in general—are meaningless.

Staff burnout can introduce a number of impediments to the effective functioning of the library. Libraries with a burnout problem may find themselves alarmingly short-staffed through increases in absenteeism, resignations, and firings. The link between burnout and turnover is well established. Some librarians have left the profession entirely, deciding to try their luck at running a craft shop or raising horses. Many more have carved new niches for themselves within the field as information brokers or consultants. Others have remained in libraries, opting for administrative careers rather than public service. Burnt-out librarians who stay on the job may withdraw from it in subtler ways—extending breaks and lunch hours, missing meetings, going home early, and routinely taking advantage of their maximum sick leave. In a library where burnout is prevalent, professional collegiality may be seriously eroded. Intra-organizational communication may break down at the informal level between coworkers, between departments, and between management and staff. An atmosphere of distrust may develop, fostering competitiveness, authority conflicts, and an insistence on doing things "by the book." If the library is unionized, the union may become involved in increasing numbers of disputes.

Burnout can also exacerbate the library's continuing fiscal dilemma. Economic analyst Robert Minnehan and psychologist Whiton Stewart Paine have identified a number of ways in which staff burnout affects organizations financially. Potential costs to the library may result from reduced employee productivity, increased sick leave, higher insurance premiums, early retirement payments, the need to recruit and orient replacement or substitute employees, provision of burnout treatment and prevention, employee sabotage, and litigation.[10] Burnout can also adversely affect library funding. Subject to both increased demands for public accountability and the scrutiny of ever more parsimonious municipal authorities, libraries may find their access to tax support seriously jeopardized if staff burnout causes noticeable declines in quality of service.

Almost inevitably the quality of service that users receive will deteriorate. The loss of energy, concern, and idealism experienced by burnt-out librarians tends to diminish their professional effectiveness. Cherniss cites research showing that teacher enthusiasm is strongly related to higher rates of student learning and that the conviction and zeal of psychotherapists are critical to healing: "Thus, although a professional's knowledge and skill are important for effective performance, his emotional state, especially the level of enthusiasm and commitment brought to the helping relationship, seems to be as important as the specific methods and techniques used."[11] The negative changes in attitude and sense of depersonalization integral to the burnout syndrome cause the professional to relate to clients as objects rather than as people. Provision of service becomes increasingly routinized, and less attention is paid to individual human needs.[12] Burnt-out librarians may develop strong antipathies to the public, considering users' questions to be unimportant or to be irritating interruptions. Users may be wrongly told that the information they need is unavailable or even deliberately given incorrect information.

**EXTENT OF THE PROBLEM**

How prevalent is librarian burnout?

Since the debut of burnout research in the mid-1970s, investigators have cast their nets ever wider, resulting in a substantial body of literature addressing a number of professional groups. Studies attest to the pervasiveness of burnout among mental health staff, day-care workers, nurses, clergymen, therapists, policemen, legal services attorneys, teachers, social workers, and others. Perhaps because of the stereotype of librarianship as a non-stressful, virtually bucolic profession, it has received scant attention from burnout researchers.

In the early eighties, interest in librarian burnout began to develop within the profession itself. Since "people work" was widely considered to be the root cause of burnout and librarianship involves high public contact, it was reasoned that librarians too might have a high susceptibility to burnout. An early study of academic reference librarians, however, suggested there might not be much cause for concern. For this study, reported in 1983, 380 questionnaires were distributed to reference librarians in seventy-five selected United States universities with enrollments of over twenty-thousand students. Of the 262 librarians who responded, only 1 percent were mild burnout, and 12 percent were burnout candidates. The study's authors concluded that "academic reference librarians do not seem to be especially prone to burnout" and speculated that since librarianship is often a second career, perhaps the librarians surveyed had experienced burnout in a previous career and had learned how to cope with stress.[13] Reassuring as these results appeared, two methodological considerations call their validity into question. First, questionnaires were not distributed to subjects directly but were sent in batches to head reference librarians, who then passed them along to staff members. This procedure may have caused subjects to doubt their anonymity and to bias their responses in a positive direction. Second, the survey instrument, the Forbes Burnout Survey, has not been widely tested and supported. In response to criticism of the study, author Nathan Smith later concluded that the results were probably too low, citing the survey instrument as the culprit.[14]

Corporate librarians were the focus of a study published the following year.[15] The Maslach Burnout Inventory was sent to 150 randomly selected corporate librarians, of whom sixty-two responded. The MBI, developed by Christina Maslach and an associate, is the most widely used index of burnout in research studies as well as in organization-sponsored workshops. It contains six subscales to measure the frequency and intensity of the three aspects of the burnout syndrome—emotional exhaustion, depersonalization, and reduced personal accomplishment. A sample item from the emotional exhaustion subscale reads "I feel emotionally drained from my work," and an item from the depersonalization subscale reads "I've become more callous toward people since I took this job."[16] Of the sixty-two respondents, twenty-nine had a high burnout score in at least one of the six subscales, and five individuals received four or more high scores. While scores related to emotional exhaustion and depersonalization were significantly lower than averaged data collected by Maslach on nurses, social workers, police officers, and teachers, librarians' scores related to reduced personal accomplishment were just as high as those of the other professional groups. Two factors were found to have a strong correlation with high burnout scores—

lack of positive feedback and a low degree of individual influence on setting library practices and policies.

In another study reported in 1984, ninety-two librarians attending a one-day conference on reference service completed the Staff Burnout Scale for Health Professionals.[17] The SBS is a thirty-item inventory developed to measure burnout as defined by Maslach and Pines and has well-established validity and reliability. Forty-eight respondents also produced drawings of their own burnout syndromes. (Projective drawings are a means of assessing subjective and possibly unconscious feelings to which a questionnaire may not be sensitive.) There was a high correlation between the results of the drawings and SBS scores. Fourteen percent (thirteen of ninety-two of the librarians were found to be "severely burned out, showing strong, sustained symptoms of continuous psychological tension." Another 28 percent (twenty-six of ninety-two) showed signs of ongoing psychological tension. Altogether, 42 percent of the sample were assessed to be at or near burnout. While the results are not generalizable because the sample was not randomly selected, the study is noteworthy both because it used a novel two-pronged approach and because it hinted at a pervasiveness of librarian burnout.

A major survey of reference librarians reported in 1986 also showed a relatively high incidence of librarian burnout.[18] For this study, 825 reference librarians employed by larger public libraries were sent the MBI together with a questionnaire that measured role ambiguity (uncertainty resulting from unclear work guidelines) and role conflict (inconsistencies related to job expectations). Usable returns numbered 547. More than 20 percent of the sample were found to have high levels of emotional exhaustion, 30 percent to have high levels of depersonalization, and 30 to 35 percent to score low in sense of personal accomplishment (low scores in this aspect indicating a high burnout level). A strong correlation existed between role strains and burnout. When the results of the study were compared with a similar survey of teachers, burnout rates of the two groups were found to be much alike.

A study of law librarians published in 1987 showed an incidence of burnout only slightly lower than that among public reference librarians.[19] Of the 119 law librarians who completed the MBI, approximately 14 percent demonstrated high levels of emotional exhaustion, and between 19 and 27 percent demonstrated high levels of depersonalization. Again, the worst scores were in the area of personal accomplishment, with about 30 percent of the sample scoring in the burnout range. As with the study of corporate librarians, the law librarians' average scores in emotional exhaustion and depersonalization were lower than the aggregate data that Maslach collected on other professions, while the personal accomplishment scores were comparable. The author remarks that while the respondents receiving high burnout scores do not represent a majority of the profession, "the presence of these high scores in the sample indicates that law librarians are not immune to burnout."

Taken together, these studies show that burnout is a problem affecting a substantial segment of the library profession. The research findings themselves may be only the tip of the iceberg. As Veneese Nelson, author of the law librarian study, points out: "Statistics can help detect a trend, but in the case of burnout, statistics tend to be less credible because a burned-out individual may not have the time or desire to return the questionnaire."[20] Further indications of the seriousness of librarian burnout can be found in the attention it attracts as a conference topic, in the proliferation of burnout seminars and workshops, and in the increasing references to the problem in the professional literature. If librarian burnout has not yet reached the stage of mass conflagration suffered by some other professional groups, it has spread far enough to jeopardize the well-being of thousands of librarians and to threaten the integrity and effectiveness of their professional practice.

## THE SEARCH FOR EXPLANATIONS AND SOLUTIONS

The underlying premise of burnout research has been that members of the human service professions are especially vulnerable to the syndrome because of the stress involved in engaging in "people work." Maslach, for example, refers to burnout as "a response to the chronic emotional strain of dealing extensively with other human beings, particularly when they are troubled or having problems."[21] But where does this approach to the burnout phenomenon leave us? How can we eliminate the cause of burnout if the cause is our professional contact with other people? Social workers without clients, teachers without students, nurses without patients, and librarians without library users cease to be social workers, teachers, nurses, and librarians.

The assumption that stress is inevitable in certain people-oriented professions has led most burnout researchers to view burnout as a problem of individual practitioners or specific work environments. Recommendations for prevention and treatment have tended to focus at this level too. Members of human service professions are advised to scrutinize themselves and colleagues for symptoms of burnout and to adopt various techniques of stress management as a means of coping with it. At the organizational level, recommended remedies include improving working conditions, fostering teamwork, and adopting flexible scheduling. While this approach may provide some symptomatic relief, it fails to address the underlying structural causes of professional burnout, and it holds little promise for discovering lasting solutions.

Those professions in which the incidence of practitioner burnout is relatively high—social work, teaching, nursing, and police work—have in common, with each other and with librarianship, their public service orientation. But they share some other characteristics which may be considerably more salient in explaining their members' high susceptibility to burnout. In the following chapter, these commonalities are examined within the context of the increasing proletarianization of professional labor. The changing nature and meaning of work, especially professional work, are considered, and a case is made for conceptualizing burnout as a manifestation of work alienation. In chapter three, the focus shifts to librarianship itself and to the factors specific to the development of the profession that have laid the kindling for alienation and burnout. Chapter four addresses several current trends and their implications for librarian alienation. In the final chapter, various strategies for coping with burnout are evaluated, with an emphasis on solutions consistent with the paradigm of burnout as alienation.

## NOTES

1. "Low Stress Ranking Rankles Librarians," *American Libraries* 17 (July-August 1986): 502–3.

2. Sarah Barbara Watstein, "Burnout: From a Librarian's Perspective" (Washington: U.S. Department of Education, 1979), p. 6.

3. Herbert J. Freudenberger, *Burnout: The High Cost of High Achievement* (New York: Anchor Press, 1980), p. 13.

4. Jerry Edelwich and Archie Brodsky, *Burn-Out: Stages of Disillusionment in the Helping Professions* (New York: Human Sciences Press, 1980), p. 14.

5. Cary Cherniss, *Professional Burnout in Human Service Organizations* (New York: Praeger, 1980), p. 5.

6. Ayala M. Pines and Elliot Aronson, *Burnout: From Tedium to Personal Growth* (New York: The Free Press, 1981), p. 15.

7. Christina Maslach, *Burnout: The Cost of Caring* (Englewood Cliffs, N.J.: Prentice-Hall, 1982), p. 3.

8. Christina Maslach, "Understanding Burnout: Definitional Issues in Analyzing a Complex Phenomenon," in *Job Stress and Burnout: Research, Theory, and Intervention Perspectives*, ed. Whiton Stewart Paine (Beverly Hills: Sage Publications, 1982), p. 32.

9. Jerome F. X. Carroll and William L. White, "Theory Building: Integrating Individual and Environmental Factors Within an Ecological Framework," in *Job Stress and Burnout*, ed. Paine, p. 44.

10. Robert F. Minnehan and Whiton Stewart Paine, "Bottom Lines: Assessing the Economic and Legal Consequences of Burnout," in *Job Stress and Burnout*, ed. Paine, p. 100.

11. Cherniss, *Professional Burnout in Human Service Organizations*, p. 8.

12. Maslach, *Burnout*, p. 78.

13. Nathan M. Smith and Veneese C. Nelson, "Burnout: A Survey of Academic Reference Librarians," *College & Research Libraries* 44 (May 1983): 245–50.

14. Veneese C. Nelson, "Burnout: A Reality for Law Librarians?" *Law Library Journal* 79 (Spring 1987): 268.

15. Nathan M. Smith and Laura F. Nielson, "Burnout: A Survey of Corporate Librarians," *Special Libraries* 75 (July 1984): 221–27.

16. Maslach, *Burnout*, p. 8.

17. Mary Haack, John W. Jones, and Tina Roose, "Occupational Burnout among Librarians," *Drexel Library Quarterly* 20 (Spring 1984): 46–72.

18. Nancy Birch, Maurice P. Marchant, and Nathan M. Smith, "Perceived Role Conflict, Role Ambiguity, and Reference Librarian Burnout in Public Libraries," *Library and Information Science Research* 8 (January-March 1986): 53–65.

19. Nelson, "Burnout," pp. 267–75.

20. Ibid., p. 274.

21. Maslach, *Burnout*, p. 3.

# 2

# Work, Alienation, and the Human Service Professions

> One of the saddest things is that the only thing a man can do for eight hours a day, day after day, is work. You can't eat eight hours a day, nor drink for eight hours a day nor make love for eight hours.
> 
> William Faulkner

## NEMESIS OR SALVATION: THE MEANING OF WORK IN WESTERN SOCIETY

Homo sapiens has long been embroiled in a love-hate affair with work. Unlike the industrious activity of our fellow beings—from hunting to honey production—human labor is based on ideas rather than instinct. Through critical reflection on the past and plans for the future, we work to transform our environment, ourselves, and each other. Equally unique, however, is our continuing ambivalence toward this means by which we remake our world.

Throughout the waxing and waning of human societies, both pre-industrial and industrial, work has remained a central fact of life. In order for basic survival needs to be met and progeny appropriately socialized, it has always been necessary that at least some members of a society work. The social organization of work and the values and meanings—ideologies—attached to it have, however, been subject to wide differentiation and to change.

To the inhabitants of ancient Greece and to their admirers, the Romans, most forms of labor were regarded as a curse. The classical Greek writings reveal a society in which nearly all productive labor, even that related to commerce and education, was performed by slaves or by the ancient equivalent of "guest workers." The free Greek citizen was under no compulsion to work for survival needs and considered such work to be inherently servile and degrading.¹ In Aristotle's *Politics*, for example, we read: "Citizens should not lead the lives of mechanics or tradesmen, for such a life is ignoble and inimical to virtue."² But while they were not expected to hoe or hew, neither did the Greeks pass their days in idleness. Relieved of the burdens of production and trade, citizens were free to perform their political duties and to pursue virtue—these being considered their proper arenas of activity. Thus a clear division of labor existed in Greek society.³

The ancient Jews, too, regarded work as a curse, but one ordained by God to punish the heirs of Adam and Eve's fateful indiscretion. Later rabbinical discourses taught that work was an element in human virtue and thus ultimately necessary for man's redemption.⁴ This latter view was adopted by medieval Christian theology, particularly with respect to members of the burgeoning monastic orders. St. Benedict established the spiritual importance of both intellectual and manual labor in his rules for the comportment of monks: "Idleness is the enemy of the soul. Therefore, the brothers should have specified periods for manual labor as well as for prayerful reading."⁵ By the late Middle Ages and Renaissance, this concept of work as virtuous and ennobling had spread to the ascendant bourgeoisie. These new men of the hour—urban merchants and artisans—perceived in work the path not only to heavenly but to earthly rewards. The comforts and pleasures made possible through financial security were no longer the sole preserve of the nobility but were not attainable for many through application to a trade. Once the new humanism gained sway, less credence was given to miracles and more to man's own ability to improve his condition through work. Some master craftsmen and merchant princes even achieved a measure of the power and prestige formerly reserved to members of the land-owning and ecclesiastical aristocracies.

Two phenomena of the sixteenth century—a rapid expansion of commerce in northern Europe and the Protestant Reformation—resulted in a consolidated ideology of work known as the Protestant ethic or, simply, the work ethic. Martin Luther introduced the concept of work as a holy calling and considered all work, mental and manual, to be of equal merit when performed to the best of the worker's abilities.⁶ Calvinist doctrine, while stating unequivocally that men are elect or doomed irrespective of their earthly acts, still prescribed a rigid pattern of behavior for the faithful to follow. In order to shore up their own confidence in being elect and to provide outward evidence of their exalted state, adherents were to be diligent in their work, eschew worldly pleasures, husband their increasing wealth carefully, and avoid the waste of time. Thus, a moral value was placed on the very characteristics necessary for commercial success, and the great wealth of nineteenth-century manufacturers was viewed as the result not of greed but of godliness. This work ethic, when applied to the working class, emphasized methodical and reliable work habits—"an internalized motivation to work hard and in a disciplined manner"—that many early factory workers lacked.[7] In his classic study, *The Protestant Ethic and the Spirit of Capitalism*, Max Weber points to the absorption of Calvinist dogma into the cultures of northern European countries and Puritan New England as a basis for the relatively greater success of industrialization in these regions.[8]

In the work ethic, then, we have a radical departure from earlier notions of work. Leisure is no longer the ideal but the enemy of virtue. Work is now the economic, social, and moral panacea, the path to individual salvation and collective civilization. In the words of nineteenth-century novelist Thomas Carlyle: "All work, even cotton spinning, is noble; work alone is noble."

## ALIENATED LABOR

> Most men would feel insulted if it were proposed to employ them in throwing stones over a wall, and then in throwing them back, merely that they might earn their wages. But many are no more worthily employed now.
>
> Henry David Thoreau

> A bad day of fishing is better than a good day of work.
>
> Bumper sticker

At the same time that the work ethic was being promulgated from pulpit and mother's knee, three socioeconomic forces came into play that would profoundly change people's attitudes toward their work. One of these forces was the rise of merchant and, then, industrial capital, concentrating the means of production in the hands of an increasingly small and dominant group. Another force was the rise of the market society. Under this system, competition became the mode of economic interaction, and profit became the ultimate determinant of the means and ends of all economic activity—the use of land and other resources, the production of goods and services, and the income and security of workers. The third of these socioeconomic forces was an increasingly elaborate division of labor. Work that previously required an individual to perform diverse mental and manual operations became fragmented into smaller and smaller tasks routinely assigned to specific workers. The division between intellectual and physical labor, that is, between conceptual organization and the performance of work, became especially pronounced.[9]

While these socioeconomic forces antedated the industrial revolution, industrialization greatly intensified their effects. Unlike the early farmers who directly produced most of the consumables their families needed or the traditional artisans who owned their tools, performed or oversaw all tasks related to their products, and sold or bartered them for their own benefit, industrial workers were totally dependent on their employers and had only their labor to sell.

Industrialization wrought at least five major changes in the relationship between workers and their work. First, the rapid expansion of urbanization and transportation brought about by the industrial revolution physically removed most people from the production of the commodities they used every day. Second, the decline of barter in favor of the universal use of money (and, more recently, credit) weakened the link between the performance of work and its rewards. Third, the tools and procedures of production became more powerful and more complex. Industrial workers did not own their tools and, in addition, they often did not understand the tools and could not control their pace. Fourth, the greatly enlarged scale of production, which required the synchronization of increasing numbers of workers, resulted in the rigid imposition of schedules. No longer could people work at times and paces that individually suited them. Work came to be defined less in terms of what was produced than in terms of hours logged on the timeclock. Finally, the efficiency imperative dictated the extreme fragmentation of work to the point that most industrial jobs required workers to use only a small fraction of their capabilities.[10]

Having steadily gathered steam throughout the nineteenth-century, industrialization charged full throttle into the twentieth. The increasing size and complexity of industrial enterprises, together with a growing product market and its attendant competition, pointed to a need for ever greater efficiency and systematization.[11] Two complementary techniques emerged to fill this need. One was the assembly line, introduced in 1914 by Henry Ford. The other was scientific management. Both of these developments extended the division of labor vertically and horizontally, thereby making work even more repetitive and monotonous.[12]

Frederick Winslow Taylor, the leading proponent of scientific management, believed that production could be boosted substantially through the application of scientific methods to the work process. He advocated an almost total separation of mental labor (management) from manual labor and the substitution of science for the worker's judgment:

Perhaps the most prominent single element in modern scientific management is the task idea. The work of every workman is fully planned out by the management at least one day in advance, and each man receives in most cases complete written instructions, describing in detail the task which he is to accomplish, as well as the means to be used in doing the work. . . . This task specifies not only what is to be done but how it is to be done and the exact time allowed for doing it.[13]

Implicit in the philosophy of scientific management—which continues to exert its influence on present-day management methods—is the assumption that workers are passive and dependent resources whose manipulation both at the hands of managers and for the greater profit of employers is appropriate and desirable. The good worker, for Taylor, was the worker who brought to the job unquestioning obedience, not critical or creative abilities.

A full half century before Taylor and Ford loosed their twin models of efficiency on the industrial scene, Karl Marx warned of the consequences of treating workers as nothing more than an exploitable resource:

Within the capitalist system all methods for raising the social productiveness of labor are brought about at the cost of the individual laborer; all means for the development of production transform themselves into means of domination over, and exploitation of, the producers; they mutilate the laborer into a fragment of a man, degrade him to the level of an appendage of a machine, destroy every remnant of charm in his work and turn it into a hated toil; they estrange from him the intellectual potentialities of the labor process in the same proportion as science is incorporated in it as an independent power.[14]

To Marx, human beings are by nature capable of reflection and have a sense of history and future. They can purposively create and produce both individually and collectively and can confront the product of their labor consciously and freely.[15] Marx viewed the history of mankind, however, as a history not only of increasing development but also of increasing alienation. His concept of alienation, like that of Hegel, is based on the distinction between man's existence and his essence.[16] Borrowing from Marx, Erich Fromm provides a concise definition of alienation:

By alienation is meant a mode of experience in which the person experiences himself as an alien. He has become, one might say, estranged from himself. He does not experience himself as the center of his world, as the creator of his own acts—but his acts and their consequences have become his masters, whom he obeys, or whom he may even worship. The alienated person is out of touch with himself as he is out of touch with any other person. He, like the others, is experienced as things are experienced; with the senses and with common sense, but at the same time without being related to oneself and to the world outside productively.[17]

Marx believes that the roots of alienation lie in work and particularly in the division of labor because work represents both the active relation between man and nature and the re-creation of both the world and humankind. As private property becomes more concentrated and the division of labor more entrenched, human labor ceases to be an expression of man's powers. Both labor and its products take on an existence separate from the worker's own will.[18] Marx outlines several ways in which workers become alienated.

Under industrial capitalism, workers generally do not produce their own sustenance directly, nor do they own the means for doing so. Instead, they sell their labor power and have, thereby, little control over the process of production and no claim to the resulting products. The producer's product is thus appropriated from him, and he is denied the opportunity to subject it to his own will. The product is subject to an alien will, that of the employer, who alone determines its purpose, content, quality, and ultimate disposition. The product takes on an existence external to and even hostile to the worker, who is thus alienated from it.[19]

Proud of my work? How can I feel pride in a job where I call a foreman's attention to a mistake, a bad piece of equipment, and he'll ignore it. Pretty soon you get the idea they don't care. You keep doing this and finally you're titled a troublemaker. So you just go about your work. You *have* to have pride. So you throw it off to something else. And that's my stamp collection. *Spot-Welder*[20]

Workers are not only alienated from their products, but they are also estranged from the act of production and, thereby, from themselves. Once individuals are coerced into selling their labor power—having no other way to make a living—they are prevented from producing freely according to their own will and consciousness; they must produce according to the demands of wills alien to themselves. In doing so, they become alienated from themselves because their very life activity belongs to someone else.[21] Work, which for Marx is the activity by which we can most clearly express our humanity, reverts to being merely the means to physical survival.[22]

God, I hated that assembly line. *I hated it*. I used to fall asleep on the job standing up and still keep doing my work. There's nothing more boring and more repetitious in the world. On top of it, you don't feel human. The machine's running you, you're not running it. *Mechanic*[23]

Workers in the capitalist mode of production become alienated from nature as well. Utterly unlike farmers who manipulate the land and other natural resources according to their own will, those who must sell their labor power to others are forced to manipulate nature as directed by their employers. The worker's own link to nature is severed.[24]

There's a lot of things I don't like about my work. I've never really appreciated seeing ground tore up. Especially if that ground could be made into something. I think about it all the time. You tear somethin' up that has taken years and years and years. *Strip Miner*[25]

The final type of alienation has to do with individuals' relationships to each other and to what Marx calls the *species life* or essential human nature. Marx argued that people who occupy different positions in the productive system—in other words, employers and workers—relate to each other in terms of pecuniary gain; their relationship is antagonistic rather than harmonious, competitive rather than cooperative. Such alienation also pervades relationships within the same class as workers are forced to compete for jobs, and owners are forced to increase their profits at the expense of competitors.[26] But the estrangement goes deeper. Under the capitalist mode of production, the entire species is prevented from living according to its natural capabilities of free and conscious creation. Individuals are denied their right to belong to a species pursuing a life congruent with its natural capabilities.[27] As Fromm summarizes: "The alienated man is not only alienated from other men; he is alienated from the essence of humanity, from his 'species-being,' both in his natural and spiritual qualities."[28]

You can work next to a guy for months without even knowing his name. One thing, you're too busy to talk. Can't hear. You have to holler in his ear. They got these little guys comin' around in white shirts and if they see you runnin' your mouth, they say, "This guy need more work." *Spot-Welder*[29]

The effects of work alienation are not sloughed off at the sound of the quitting bell. Feelings of powerlessness and meaninglessness permeate all of the arenas in which people live their lives. Ultimately, alienation leads to the erosion and even perversion of human values. Marx believed that when economic values—working hard, being thrifty, amassing wealth—become the supreme aim in life, man is unable to develop moral values.[30]

Under alienating conditions, true human needs become difficult to identify and satisfy. As alienated individuals relate to each other as means rather than as ends, they continually try to implant other new needs, which they can then gratify for their own economic gain: "No eunuch flatters his tyrant more shamefully or seeks by more infamous means to stimulate his jaded appetite, in order to gain some favor, than does the eunuch of industry, the entrepreneur, in order to acquire a few silver coins or to charm the gold from the purse of his dearly beloved neighbor."[31] German philosopher Herbert Marcuse refers to these artificially instilled desires as false needs:

"False" are those which are superimposed upon the individual by particular social interests in his repression: the needs which perpetuate toil, aggressiveness, misery, and injustice. . . . Most of the prevailing needs to relax, to have fun, to behave and consume in accordance with the advertisements, to love and hate what others love and hate, belong to this category of false needs.[32]

As individuals become increasingly wrapped up in satisfying these false needs, they come to relate to the rest of the world almost wholly in terms of consumption. Marx wrote, "The less you *are*, the less you express your life, the more you *have*, the greater is your *alienated* life."[33] Alienation causes individuals to perceive and use physical objects, natural resources, art, education, religion, and other people as expendable commodities. Nor is the self exempt from this process. Fromm refers to the relationship of alienated individuals to themselves as "marketing orientation." Alienated from their human powers, individuals do not experience themselves as active and effective participants in the world but as commodities to be employed as successfully as possible on the market.[34] This misapprehension of self as external object is well understood by the Madison Avenue advertising executive responsible for the automobile commercial that opens: "If you accept the basic premise that you are what you drive. . . ."

Harmful as the consequences of alienation are for the individual, the consequences for society at large are more disturbing. Marcuse argues that alienated individuals become "swallowed up" by their alienated existence. The satisfaction of preconditioned needs is superficially pleasurable, bringing consumers and producers together in a generally amicable collaboration. Eventually, no other way of life seems desirable or even imaginable:

The products indoctrinate and manipulate; they promote a false consciousness which is immune against its falsehood. And as these beneficial products become available to more individuals in more social classes, the indoctrination they carry ceases to be publicity; it becomes a way of life. It is a good way of life—much better than before—and as a good way of life, it militates against qualitative change. Thus emerges a pattern of *one-dimensional thought and behavior* in which ideas, aspirations, and objectives that, by their content, transcend the established universe of discourse and action are either repelled or reduced to terms of this universe.[35]

Thus, the routinization of our alienated state leads to the "repression of the awareness of the basic problems of human existence," undermining any hopes for their solution.[36] Estranged from our own conscious and creative powers, from the fruits of our labor, from each other, and from our collective human essence, we are held in thrall by the dehumanizing forces which we have unwittingly given domination over us.

In the Marxist view, alienation is not a vague synonym for the "human condition" as it has come to be understood in latter twentieth-century popular culture. It is, instead, a concrete term for problems brought about through identifiable and historically specific social structural settings.[37] As such, the Marxist concept of alienation remains a useful analytical instrument and will constitute the definition for alienation throughout this book. Inherent within a historically specific model of alienation is the recognition that existing conditions are susceptible to human intervention.

## LUNCH PAIL AND BRIEFCASE: TWO TRADITIONAL MODELS OF WORK

While some manual labor is both well paid and intrinsically satisfying—mainly in the skilled trades—most is neither. The majority of blue-collar workers are chronic victims of economic insecurity. Many hourly workers, especially in the service sector, are members of the "working poor"; even though they hold down full-time jobs, they cannot afford a reasonable standard of living. Fluctuations in the economy, advancing technology, and the shift of production to less expensive labor pools in the third world have made the fear of layoff and of permanent job loss a fact of life in most working-class families. A substantial proportion of blue-collar workers lack paid vacations, sick leave, and pension plans.

Nor are economic woes the worst feature of working-class life. Most blue-collar jobs require little skill or training, with the result that workers do, indeed, resemble easily replaceable cogs in the machinery. Blue-collar workers have little hope for advancement. To become skilled in trades, individuals must either go to school or arrange an apprenticeship, both generally requiring a commitment early in their career. Not only are most forms of manual labor physically exhausting, but many blue-collar workplaces expose workers to health and safety hazards, whether from excessive noise, toxic materials, heavy machinery, or video display terminals.

Most damaging, perhaps, is the laborer's forced surrender of freedom and autonomy. Blue-collar workers typically cannot arrange their work schedules to accommodate personal obligations or crises, and they cannot modify the pace of work to suit individual needs or inclinations. Most blue-collar jobs are entirely defined and directed by someone other than the worker. A common complaint of workers is that bosses regard them as unintelligent and refuse to consider their suggestions for improving work procedures. Often, behaviors that are only indirectly related to the job are regulated as well, for example, horseplay, loitering, or insubordination.[38] Blue-collar workers are often subject to punishments meted out by management, including layoffs, cutbacks in overtime, and docked salaries, and they lack due process.

Manual labor, while economically indispensable, is generally assigned a low social value and little, if any, prestige. To be a blue-collar worker, typically, is to be economically vulnerable, to have little upward mobility, and to lack choice and autonomy. In her study of fifty working class families, sociologist Lillian Rubin found bitterness, boredom, alienation, and resignation to be the defining features of their work experience. Work represented not a potential source of satisfaction and fulfillment, but merely "hours to be gotten through until you can go home."[39]

Traditionally, professional work—involving discretion and judgment by the worker, relative lack of standardization, and high levels of training—has stood in sharp contrast to manual labor. Ideally, in professional work the worker's pace, the workplace conditions, the product, the use of the product, and even to a degree its price are largely determined by the worker.[40] To be a professional is to belong to an occupational elite. The term itself, however, has acquired a plethora of connotations that detract from its usefulness as an analytical concept. We have, for example, professional football players, carpets and swimming pools that are professionally installed, and "the world's oldest profession."

Until the Renaissance, the term *profession* referred to something that was professed, an avowal or an expression of intention or purpose. This usage stemmed from the taking of consecrated vows. By the sixteenth century, the word profession was used to refer to the university educated occupations of divinity, law, and medicine, reflecting the clerical foundations of the medieval university.[41] The association of these professions with the Church, together with their use of Latin, increased the aura of mystery and authority surrounding the body of esoteric knowledge on which they were based.[42] Early practitioners of divinity, law, and medicine were almost exclusively members of aristocratic or, at least, wealthy families. It has, indeed, been suggested that the high prestige accorded to the professions originated more in the status of those who filled their ranks than in a respect for the skills and activities involved in their practice.[43] The French Revolution and, to a greater extent, the industrial revolution served to democratize the social composition of the professions. While the offspring of laborers rarely aspired so high, the progeny of the middle classes were quick to seize this opportunity for social mobility.

In addition to the high status and prestige accorded to members of the professions, they have also traditionally enjoyed a privileged position vis-à-vis the economy. Despite the laissez-faire philosophy that has so strongly influenced domestic economic policies in the United States, the established professions have been legally exempted from competition—that is, only individuals credentialed by the professions themselves can prepare wills or perform surgery for compensation. This political sanction has in turn granted the professions an authority and power far beyond the scope of other occupations.

Motivated in part, perhaps, by the status, prestige, power, and economic invulnerability attached to the professions, members of other occupational groups began to desire similar recognition and protection. The resulting professionalization movements of the nineteenth century were both swift and widespread. In the forty-year span between 1847 and 1887, no fewer than eleven professional associations of national scope were established, including, in addition to physicians and lawyers, teachers, architects, social workers, and librarians.[44]

On what grounds do the professions stake their claim to unique privilege? How, precisely, does professional work differ from other, less prestigious occupations? A general answer is that society grants these rewards 1) because the professions have special competence deriving from esoteric knowledge, and this competence is essential to meeting societal needs and supporting societal values and 2) because the professions are committed to ethical public service, their motivation being altruistic rather than materialistic.

Much has been written on the attributes of professions, nineteenth- and early twentieth-century commentators emphasizing the virtue and nobility of professions, while more recent analyses have criticized their monopolistic position and questioned the authenticity of their selfless dedication. There is a surprising consensus, however, on certain structural and attitudinal characteristics that distinguish the professions from other occupations and that, taken together, provide a model of professionalism. The structural requirements of a profession are: 1) that it be a full-time occupation, not a sideline or avocation; 2) that it be based on a specialized body of knowledge and techniques; 3) that it have its own training institutions, controlled by members; 4) that it have an established association that defines membership and provides self-regulatory mechanisms; 5) that it be licensed or certified by a legal authority; 6) that it be recognized by the community; and 7) that it have a code of ethics to justify the privilege of autonomy and self-governance. Equally important to the professional paradigm are several attitudinal components. Professionals are expected 1) to have a sense of commitment and identification with the professional association; 2) to have a selfless desire to serve the public; and 3) to feel they were called to their work. Professionals also typically believe that rigorous professional education and self-imposed quality standards make external regulation unnecessary and that their work deserves high rewards, both material and subjective.[45]

## THE PROLETARIANIZATION OF PROFESSIONAL WORK

The number of professional workers in America quadrupled between 1900 and 1950.[46] Their authority, both imputed and real, also escalated rapidly so that, by mid-century, professionals were being hailed as a dominant new social class. In 1968, influential American sociologist Talcott Parsons unequivocally pronounced: "The massive emergence of the professional complex, not the special status of capitalistic or socialistic modes or organization, is the crucial structural development in twentieth-century society."[47] Daniel Bell, the formulator of post-industrial theory, accorded professionals pride of place in his analysis as well. Bell argues that, in the coming post-industrial social order, knowledge will replace capital as the central economic factor and that the possessors of knowledge will supersede the possessors of capital as figures of power and control.[48] Even the outspoken critic of American professions, Ivan Illich, does not question the formidability of their authority: "They are more deeply entrenched than a Byzantine bureaucracy, more international than a world church, more stable than any labor union, endowed with wider competencies than any shaman, and equipped with a tighter hold over those they claim as victims than any mafia."[49]

This view of professionals as powerful personages is widely shared by their patients, clients, students, parishioners, and others. But while professionals often intervene in people's lives with great authority—receiving privileged information, allocating money and benefits, even making life-and-death decisions—their own autonomy is undergoing a steady erosion. During the same half century that the number of American professionals quadrupled, the number of salaried professionals increased tenfold. This employment pattern has intensified since World War II, with the result that the self-employed now represent a minority in nearly all the professions.[50] Thus, the doctor with his impressive black bag has become a team member at a large medical center, while the family lawyer now reports each morning to the probate department of a downtown law firm.

The current demise of the entrepreneurial professional has been likened to the proletarianization of craft workers.[51] This tendency can be seen as early as the fifteenth century, when, to protect their membership from increasingly keen competition, the guilds attached such rigid economic specifications to attaining the position of mastercraftsman that a permanent class of journeymen arose. It was in the wake of the industrial revolution, however, that the craftsman's traditionally autonomous mode of work became most severely compromised. Increasing mechanization, together with rapid shifts in market conditions and the flow of capital, deepened craft workers' dependence on merchants for both financial underwriting and the ultimate marketing of their products. As the requirements for transportation and coordination necessitated centralized workplaces, more and more craftsmen became factory employees, experiencing the same loss of control over their work process and products as other proletarian workers.

The conversion of relatively independent professionals to salaried employees can be seen as the result of three contemporary structural factors.[52] First, technological development, while spurring the demand for highly trained labor, has proven to be the same stumbling block to individual professional enterprise as it did to autonomous craft production a century ago. It is the rare physician who can afford to equip his or her office with a CAT scanner. Engineers, scientists, journalists, researchers, and other professionals have become dependent on institutions whose scales of operation are large enough to permit the maintenance of state-of-the-art information technology. As this technology becomes increasingly crucial to the practice of various professions, the institutions that own and control it hold increasing sway over those who use it. A second factor is the very expansion of professional services and the markets for them. Satisfying the needs of mass clienteles necessitates administrative and organizational resources generally beyond the capacity of individual practitioners. Once large-scale operations have absorbed certain professional functions, professional dependency is increased.

Solo practitioners are then driven out of the marketplace as they are unable to compete with the economies of scale enjoyed by corporations or government agencies. Both of these structural factors are rooted in the third factor, which is the flow of capital into the knowledge and service sectors. As profit margins continue to decline in the industrial sector, this flow has become a flood, sweeping along with it the professional markets, which then become mere divisions of giant corporate markets. Caught in the undertow are professional workers, whose professional autonomy becomes subordinate to the corporate and public bureaucracies that now employ them.

Confident post-industrial visions of the ascendant professional have failed to consider—or, at least, they underestimate—the confounding role of the modern bureaucracy. An accurate assessment of professional autonomy is dependent on an understanding of the distinction between people who manage and those who are managed, between technocrats and technicians.[53] Bureaucracy means, literally, "rule by the office" or "rule by officials." While bureaucratic settings differ in the degree to which they conform to the Weberian ideal type (characterized by rationality in decision making, impersonality in social relations, routinization of tasks, and centralization of authority),[54] they inevitably impose on their employees certain constraints that result in a conflict between managerial authority and professional authority. In this battle of wills, the dependent professional rarely emerges victorious. Sociologist C. Wright Mills, in his classic monograph, *White Collar*, portrays the role of professional workers as shrinking to that of cogs in the bureaucratic hierarchy:

> They work in some department, under some kind of manager; while their salaries are often high, they are salaries, and the conditions of their work are laid down by rule. What they work on is determined by others, even as they determine how a host of sub-professional assistants will work. Thus they themselves become part of the managerial demiurge.[55]

Bureaucracies tend to replicate, for their professional employees, factory-like conditions, including fixed jurisdictions, hierarchical chains of command, internal mobility based upon performance of uniform tasks, and extensive division of labor.[56] The tendency to increase and rigidify the division of labor has two principal effects. First, more routine tasks are delegated to lower-level workers, and, second, lateral specialization of functions occurs at various levels.[57] While the specialized skills that remain within the individual's sphere of operation may be highly valued and rewarded by the bureaucracy, the professional job itself has undergone de-skilling. And the skills themselves may lose value on the market as narrow specialization both increases the risk of one's skills becoming routinized and obsolescent and reduces the opportunity for broadening one's professional expertise. The academic librarian who spends the day processing engineering texts, for example, may lose touch with other literatures, thus becoming at the same time less versatile in terms of marketable skills and more dependent on the present employer. Further, as professional employees increase their degree of specialization, they often decrease their chances for career advancement. Large-scale bureaucracies tend to maintain a "dual ladder of promotion": the technical or professional route is limited by the role one's specific set of skills plays in the organization, while the managerial route leads ultimately to decision making.[58]

Another tendency of bureaucratic employers, again with obvious parallels to the factory assembly line, is the intensification of the labor process. In government agencies, this speeding up is often the result of or, at any rate, is ascribed to increasing public demands for accountability. While the petty tyrannies of the timeclock are rarely applied to professional workers, caseloads can be made heavier, in-baskets filled more frequently, or six patients scheduled each hour instead of four. Overburdened professionals may respond at first by working longer hours, but this strategy is self-limiting. Eventually, intensification can lead to the erosion of professional standards as more and more corners are cut to keep up with the pace of work. Professional development suffers in direct relation to the decrease in time for continuing education and professional reading. A more ambiguous result of intensification is the unlooked-for gain in polyvalence experienced by some overworked professional employees. In a bureaucratic setting characterized by chronic work overload, personnel shortages must often be covered by employees who must learn new skills to handle their new responsibilities.[59] This situation is common in high schools, where a teacher of history may suddenly be confronted with a class of biology students. Another example can be seen in the 1987 reorganization of the Metro Toronto Reference Library. Reference librarians previously assigned to specific subject departments now staff, in rota, reference desks serving several different subject departments. While these librarians will doubtless increase their skills in other subject areas, they may well lose ground in their chosen areas of expertise.

Professional employees of bureaucratic organizations are, as might be expected, highly susceptible to role strains of various kinds. Role overload is experienced as a result of intensification, wherein so many demands are made on professional workers that it becomes impossible for them to meet all their responsibilities. Role conflict occurs when the worker is subject to demands that are inherently incompatible. A librarian assigned temporarily to another branch to oversee the installation of a new automated system, for example, may, once there, be expected to spend time answering reference questions or doing other routine work. A major source of role conflict lies in the disparity between organizational goals and professional ideals. Teachers who are personally committed to encouraging their students to be creative and innovative may experience conflict over imposing exams, grades, and classroom discipline. Role ambiguity occurs when the professional worker lacks adequate information to perform effectively. It may result from lack of clarity regarding the scope of the job, absence of feedback from supervisors or colleagues, or being out of touch with decision making at the organizational level.

The worklife of even highly educated and well-paid bureaucratic employees stands in sharp contrast to that of professionals engaged in private practice. While professionals have never been entirely free agents, having always had to contend with the constraints of both the marketplace and the law, their control over their own time, technical procedures, remuneration, and even professional goals has traditionally distinguished them from industrial workers. The assimilation of professionals into public and private bureaucracies has blurred this distinction. Professional workers have come to resemble industrial workers in their dependent status, in their surrender of control over the pace and technical aspects of their work, and, perhaps most significantly, in their subordination to organizational goals. The leveling, deskilling, and routinization of the bureaucracy have largely proletarianized professional work and have also greatly increased professional workers' susceptibility to what had been considered an almost exclusively proletarian malaise—alienation.

When an individual, whether carpenter or psychiatrist, must sell his or her labor in order to earn a living, alienation is inherent in the transaction. For professional employees, just as for industrial workers, the loss of control over time and task serves to estrange them from their work. Professionals' skills are foremost among the tools of their trade and are their means of production. When these skills are placed at the disposal of the modern bureaucracy, not only are they degraded through specialization and routinization (so that the professional's bargaining power is reduced in the labor market), but they must be exercised to further the interests of the bureaucracy rather than the personal or professional interests of the worker. In Marxist terms, the professional's skills have been subject to an alien will and thus appropriated. A twenty-eight-year-old editor describes her relationship to her work:

Jobs are not big enough for people. It's not just the assembly line worker whose job is too small for his spirit, you know? A job like mine, if you really put your spirit into it, you would sabotage immediately. You don't dare. So you absent your spirit from it. My mind has been so divorced from my job, except as a source of income, it's really absurd.[60]

The final step in the proletarianization of professional work is unionization. White-collar unions, like their blue-collar counterparts, have arisen in response to work alienation.[61] Bureaucratic deskilling has left many professional workers with a field of expertise so narrowed that it can no longer serve as a base of power and control within the organization.[62] Accompanying this process is a deep erosion of professional prestige. Professional workers in this situation are turning increasingly to political action as their last defense against powerlessness. Professional societies and associations originally established for such purposes as learned exchange now engage in collective bargaining. Many professionals have also joined trade unions, whose rank-and-file memberships may be all professional or may include allied manual workers.

### Semi-Professionals

One of the first sociologists to examine social stratification within the professional context, Amitai Etzioni angered many teachers, nurses, social workers, and others by his contention that they do not "deserve" full professional status and should cease trying to "pass" as something they are not.[63] While his analysis is often clouded by condescension, his definition of the semi-professions is clear: "Their training is shorter, their status is less legitimated, their right to privileged communication less established, there is less of a specialized body of knowledge, and they have less autonomy from supervision or societal control than 'the' professions."[64]

While the other criteria are arguable, it is certainly true that those workers classed as semi-professionals enjoy even less autonomy in their work than do "fully-fledged" professionals. A common bond among teachers, nurses, social workers—and librarians—is that they have no historical tradition as free practitioners. With few exceptions, they have always worked as employees of schools, hospitals, government or private agencies, and libraries. Unlike members of the established professions, such as medicine and law, or even the new professions, such as engineering, semi-professionals owe their occupational identity and functions to bureaucratic organizations. Their defenses against bureaucratic proletarianization are thus commensurately more fragile than those of professionals entering bureaucracies with the backing of tradition and the authority of a long-established and independently validated knowledge base.[65]

The proletarianization of semi-professional work has proceeded apace with the increasing scale of public and private bureaucracies. Even the ongoing struggles toward professionalism among teachers, nurses, and similar occupational groups have not served to check this encroachment. In fact, while professionalism has long been considered a route to increased autonomy, upward mobility, and status by members of the semi-professions, it has in reality been less instrumental in their behalf than in the interests of the bureaucratic organizations for which they work. An important tenet of the professional ideology of social work, for example, is neutrality. Professional social workers are expected to suspend their own personal, ethical, and political values and to identify instead with the aims and principles of their agencies.[66] This neutrality imperative, in addition to discouraging overidentification or emotional involvement with the client, also militates against social workers' interests as workers. If what is good for the agency is good for the staff, how can staff members then be so unprofessional as to challenge the agency's prerogatives through collective bargaining? This manipulation of the ideology of professionalism in favor of management has also been observed among health care workers:

> For the unskilled and semiskilled workers, there are forces which lead to a kind of passive alienation from the content of their work. For the skilled workers, there is the ideology of professionalism. The first denies the service ethic and accepts the class division in the hospital. The second denies the class division and diverts the service ethic into a professional ethic of institutional loyalty. . . . Skilled workers are seduced by the ideology of professionalism into foregoing both qualitative and quantitative satisfactions in return for an abstract sense of status.[67]

## BURNOUT AS ALIENATION

Despite murmurs of middle-class disaffection in the fifties and rumbles of white-collar woe in the sixties and seventies, the emergence of professional burnout was a largely unanticipated phenomenon. No ready-made explanations for it existed in either the professional paradigms or in social theory. Beyond its apparent concentration in certain occupational groups, few patterns could at first be discerned.

Much of the research and commentary in the literature of burnout has been concerned with isolating the factors responsible for the phenomenon. A number of work-related stresses have been implicated. Some researchers have targeted "people work" itself as the key stress leading to burnout. As Maslach puts it, "People pay a heavy price for being their brother's (and sister's) keeper."[68] A related strain, experienced by most human service professionals at some time during their careers, is the imbalance between the needs and expectations of clients and the availability of resources and skills to meet them. Other researchers have focused on variables relating to specific work settings. Social psychologist Ayala M. Pines, for example, argues that "even the same person, working with people exhibiting similar problems in two organizations similar in function, budget, and sociopolitical environment, may burn out in one and not in the other."[69] The organizational stresses most frequently cited as factors in burnout are lack of autonomy, role strains, long hours, insufficient time out or time off, isolation, physically unpleasant work environments, lack of feedback from clients and supervisors, lack of collegial support, administrative indifference or excessive interference, public misapprehension of the nature and/or significance of the work, excessive demands for productivity, tedium, inadequate opportunities for personal and professional growth, and inadequate rewards in the form of salary, prestige, or career advancement.

Most analyses of burnout view the problem as arising not from situational variables alone, however, but from the interaction between these and individual personality variables. Maslach, while arguing convincingly that the organizational determinants of burnout must be examined—"Imagine investigating the personality of cucumbers to discover why they had turned into sour pickles without analyzing the vinegar barrels in which they had been submerged!"[70]—believes, nonetheless, that the cucumbers too should come in for their share of scrutiny:

What a person brings to a situation is just as critical as what the situation brings out of (or puts into) him or her. And what a person brings are individual characteristics such as motivations, needs, values, self-esteem, emotional expressiveness and control, and personal style. These internal qualities determine how someone handles external sources of emotional stress and help explain why Person A will experience burnout in a particular setting while Person B will not.[71]

Maslach sums up the "burnout personality" as an individual who is weak and unassertive in dealing with people, is impatient and intolerant, lacks self-confidence, has little ambition, and tends to be reserved and conventional.[72] Psychologist Cary Cherniss, another pioneer writer in the area of burnout, contends that while any work setting that is high in role conflict and ambiguity, low in autonomy and variety, and subject to poor management will induce burnout in its occupants, five specific personality traits greatly increase an individual's vulnerability. These are: neurotic anxiety, the "Type A" syndrome, an "external" locus of control (fatalism), flexibility, and introversion.[73] In a less clinical but similar vein, Charles Zastrow concludes that burnout is caused by two types of factors: distressing events and "certain kinds of self-defeating thoughts about distressing events."[74]

Other researchers have viewed burnout as primarily a personality disorder. Herbert J. Freudenberger, psychoanalyst and industrial consultant, considers three personality types to be susceptible to burnout. The first of these is the dedicated worker who feels highly pressured both to achieve and to meet the needs of his or her clients. The second personality type is overcommitted; these workers have overinvested emotionally in their careers to compensate for lacks in other areas of their lives. The third personality type is the authoritarian, the individual with a neurotic need for control.[75] Harvey J. Fischer, another psychoanalyst, also identifies the potential burnout personality as overly dedicated to his or her work. He contends, further, "that these people lead shallow lives, and while we therefore might not want them as friends, we might well seek to hire such extraordinarily dedicated people to work for us."[76] According to Fischer, individuals vulnerable to burnout have organized their entire lives around their work, and, when frustration or setbacks occur, these individuals respond by redoubling their efforts. The motive for such desperation is described as the pursuit of the "illusion of grandiosity": "These pursuers have gone beyond reasonableness, common sense, and concern for health and well-being."[77]

With few exceptions, the literature on burnout situates the responsibility for the problem within the individual practitioner, within the specific institution or agency for which the individual works, or in some kind of interaction between the two. Several reasons for the predominance of this level of analysis can be identified. First, symptoms of burnout do appear in individuals. Explanations based on personality variables have the virtue of dealing with the otherwise thorny question of why one nurse burns out while another nurse, working in the same hospital unit and presumably under the same pressure, does not. Second, professional workers are still thought of as relatively autonomous—in charge of their careers and only minimally subject to external control. If they become dysfunctional, it is tempting to conclude that this result also has an individual basis. The tendency to consider burnout as a result of personality traits or individual pathology is also in keeping with the psychiatric world view that developed along with the rapid expansion of the professional class in the 1940s. This ideology, compatible with an increasingly individualistic and competitive society, assigned psychological diagnoses to individuals beset by social, educational, or economic problems, largely ignoring and thus deflecting attention from any structural antecedents.[78] Broadening the analysis of burnout to the level of the particular organizational unit represents not a shift in approach from a pathological to a social structural perspective but only a slight enlargement of focus from individual to group pathology. Thus, a work setting "marked by intrastaff hostility" has been contrasted with one in which "the work atmosphere was supportive and exciting," the former being considered more likely to produce a high burnout rate.[79]

The complex problem of how to prevent and treat burnout has also imposed constraints on the level of analysis. Change, even at the organizational level, is frequently considered a daunting proposition:

Unfortunately one cannot count on an organization to take remedial action. Occasionally an extremely enlightened organization may accomplish this task, but this is a rare exception. . . . Some aspects of a bureaucracy simply *cannot* be changed.[80]

Even more formidable is the prospect of effecting structural change. The comparative simplicity of developing and applying individual strategies for coping with burnout—even if these are only minimally effective—has deflected attention from social structural causes and solutions.

Analytically, it is more fruitful to conceptualize burnout as a manifestation of work alienation than as a problem of individuals and particular work settings. Howard Karger, one of the few writers on the subject to equate burnout with alienation, reminds us that the framing of research questions and the assumptions underlying them necessarily impose limitations and boundaries on our conclusions.[81] Research and discussion on burnout have proceeded from events occurring in limited and even subjective contexts: the burning out of individual employees. Investigation has thus focused primarily on the burnt-out individual and his or her immediate environment rather than on the search for deeper or broader explanations. Another limiting factor has been the traditional assumption that professional workers enjoy significantly more autonomy in their work than do industrial laborers. Alienation has rarely been considered a component of professional worklife. The degree to which professional—and, even more, semi-professional—work has been proletarianized, however, has greatly increased professional workers' susceptibility to alienation. If we set aside these limiting assumptions, it becomes clear that burnout and work alienation are very closely associated, if not the same phenomenon.

Almost 150 years ago Marx described the subjective experience of alienated labor as

external to the worker . . . it is not part of his nature; and that, consequently, he does not fulfill himself in his work but denies himself, has a feeling of misery rather than well-being, does not develop freely his mental and physical energies but is physically exhausted and mentally debased. The worker, therefore, feels himself at home only during his leisure time, whereas at work he feels homeless. His work is not voluntary but imposed, *forced labor*. It is not the satisfaction of a need, but only a *means* for satisfying other needs.[82]

Marx's observations are remarkably congruent with the descriptions of burnout developed by leading researchers in the field. Pines and Aronson refer to burnout as a state of "physical, emotional, and mental exhaustion . . . characterized by physical depletion, by feelings of helplessness and hopelessness, by emotional drain, and by the development of negative self-concept and negative attitudes toward work, life, and other people."[83] Maslach considers burnout to be "one type of job stress," involving a syndrome of emotional exhaustion, depersonalization, and reduced personal accomplishment.[84] Cherniss characterizes burnout as "psychological withdrawal from work in response to excessive stress or dissatisfaction. . . . One no longer lives to work but works only to live."[85]

The major determinant of work alienation is lack of autonomy. When individuals, of necessity, well their labor, they lose control over most technical and administrative dimensions of their work. Because, as Marx argued, work represents our main means of personal creative development, alienated workers also become estranged from other basic aspects of life.[86] Lack of autonomy is also emerging as a major causal variable in the empirical research on job stress.

In their 1972 review study of previous research on organizational stress, French and Caplan found a number of stresses to be associated with low job satisfaction and/or job-related threat to workers' well-being. These included poor relations with others, role conflict, role ambiguity, and quantitative and qualitative overload. Of all the stresses identified, however, low employee participation in decisions affecting their work had the greatest harmful effect.[87] Further, when the level of participation was held constant, the correlations of all the other stresses to job satisfaction and to job-related threat declined significantly. French and Caplan concluded that low participation in fact generates poor collegial relations, role strains, and overload as well as low job satisfaction and high job-related threat to well-being.[88] More recent research has supported French and Caplan's findings that low participation in decision making—lack of autonomy—is a primary job stress. In a 1984 study of 161 women employed by a large state social service agency, a significant relationship was found between feelings of job tension and limited opportunity for independent decision making. This study is interesting in that the subjects were predominantly white, middle-class, well-educated, middle-aged women—not unlike the demographic makeup of the library profession.[89] A 1985 study investigated a number of stresses experienced by teachers. Particularly high degrees of stress were reported for events over which the teachers had little control and which were usually the responsibility of management.[90] In a study of nurses and other hospital workers, increased participation was found both to reduce levels of role conflict and ambiguity and to increase workers' perception of control over and satisfaction with their job.[91] Position in the bureaucratic hierarchy has also been found to play an important role in job stress. Canadian sociologist James Rinehart contends that managers, generally speaking, "are structurally less prone to alienation than most other workers because of the scope of their jobs and their capacity to make decisions."[92] In a large survey of social workers employed by private and public agencies, hospitals, community mental health centers, and universities, it was found that, across all job settings, "workers" comprised the highest proportion of the high-stress category (62.6 percent), followed by administrators (22.6 percent) and supervisors (14.6 percent). Presumably, the workers would have had the lowest level of autonomy.[93]

Other research has investigated the relationship between autonomy and burnout itself. A 1987 study of mental health professionals concluded that work environments demanding high personal adherence to work through restrictions on workers' freedom or flexibility are associated with high levels of burnout.[94] Among a group of professionals in the fields of college student personnel, health, mental health, administration, and others, feelings of control over various job characteristics were negatively correlated with burnout. Demographic variables had no effect on burnout nor did number of hours worked or being on call.[95] In a study of corporate librarians, the "amount of influence the individual has on setting library policies and practices" was strongly related to burnout scores.[96]

Arising from the same source—lack of autonomy—work alienation and burnout produce, in turn, the same major effects. While the reactions of individuals to alienating conditions can take a variety of forms, the more dominant response has been characterized as fatalistic or noninvolving.[97] Similarly, withdrawal is a defining characteristic of the burnout syndrome.[98] Various physiological disorders as well as decreased satisfaction in interpersonal relationships have been attributed to both alienation and burnout. Attitudinal responses to burnout include "expressions of hopelessness, powerlessness, meaninglessness," which also represent major dimensions of alienation.[99] Several signs of staff burnout within the work environment have been identified: a significant decrement in quality of services provided to clients or customers; increased authority conflicts; poor staff morale; increased formality; increased absenteeism; and higher turnover.[100] Worker alienation is similarly reflected in absenteeism, increased numbers of grievances, turnover, and diminished productivity.[101]

There seems little justification for continuing to view burnout as qualitatively distinct from the broader concept of work alienation. Burnout has taken its greatest toll among those professions that have traditionally been most dependent upon bureaucratic organizations and have thus been most vulnerable to bureaucratic forms of control and proletarianization. The definitions, causes, and effects of burnout duplicate those of work alienation. One question remains, however. If burnout is a manifestation of work alienation, and all those who sell their labor are subject to such alienation, then why do some people burn out and not others? To be sure, some people are more alienated in their work than others. But more to the point is that alienation is not always experienced consciously:

Through many years of doing what they "must" do instead of what they *want* to do, and behaving as they "must" behave instead of as they would *like* to behave, most people come to accept the "natural order" of things. It is possible that under these conditions workers are alienated, but that their alienation is unconscious.[102]

It is perhaps most accurate to consider burnout as a process of becoming aware of one's alienated state and of the feelings of powerlessness, meaninglessness, normlessness, isolation, and self-estrangement that comprise it. The specific events that trigger the process in an individual, like all final straws, have relatively little analytical significance.

Is this just a semantic quibble? Does it really matter whether we call a librarian "burnt-out" or "alienated"? Individual problems imply individual solutions, while structural problems imply structural ones. If we continue to regard burnout as a problem of individual practitioners and particular organizational units, our attempts at prevention and treatment will remain focused at that level. In fact, individual coping strategies have been found to have little effect in reducing work-related stress.[103] Conceptualizing burnout as a manifestation of work alienation provides not only an increased scope for understanding the phenomenon but a sounder theoretical basis for evaluating potential solutions.

**NOTES**

1. Walter S. Neff, *Work and Human Behavior*, 3rd ed. (New York: Aldine, 1985), p. 33.
2. Aristotle, quoted in Bertrand Russell, *A History of Western Philosophy* (New York: Simon & Schuster, 1972), p. 192.
3. P. D. Anthony, *The Ideology of Work* (London: Tavistock, 1977), p. 15.
4. Michael Rose, *Re-Working the Work Ethic: Economic Values and Socio-Cultural Politics* (New York: Schocken Books, 1985), p. 28.
5. Timothy Fry, ed., *The Rule of St. Benedict: In Latin and English with Notes* (Collegeville, Minn.: Liturgical Press, 1981), p. 249.
6. Rose, *Re-Working the Work Ethic*, p. 30.
7. Nicholas Abercrombie, Stephen Hill, and Bryan S. Turner, *The Dominant Ideology Thesis* (London: George Allen & Unwin, 1980), p. 101.
8. Rose, *Re-Working the Work Ethic*, p. 31.
9. James W. Rinehart, *The Tyranny of Work: Alienation and the Labour Process*, 2nd ed. (Toronto: Harcourt, Brace Jovanovich Canada, 1987), pp. 19–21.
10. Sar A. Levitan and Clifford M. Johnson, *Second Thoughts on Work* (Kalamazoo, Mich.: W. E. Upjohn Institute for Employment Research, 1982), pp. 24–25.
11. W. J. Heisler, "Worker Alienation: 1900–1975," in *A Matter of Dignity: Inquiries into the Humanization of Work,* ed. W. J. Heisler and John W. Houck (Notre Dame, Ind.: University of Notre Dame Press, 1977), p. 66.
12. Rinehart, *The Tyranny of Work*, p. 52.
13. Frederick Winslow Taylor, *The Principles of Scientific Management* (New York: Harper and Brothers, 1919), p. 39.
14. Karl Marx, *Capital*, vol. 1 (New York: Modern Library, 1906), p. 708.
15. Isidor Walliman, *Estrangement: Marx's Conception of Human Nature and the Division of Labor* (Westport, Conn.: Greenwood Press, 1981), p. 31.
16. Erich Fromm, *Marx's Concept of Man* (New York: Ungar, 1961), p. 47.
17. Erich Fromm, *The Sane Society* (New York: Rinehart, 1955), pp. 120–21.
18. Fromm, *Marx's Concept of Man*, p. 47.
19. Walliman, *Estrangement*, pp. 31–32.
20. Studs Terkel, *Working: People Talk About What They Do All Day and How They Feel About What They Do* (New York: Pantheon Books, 1972), p. 162.
21. Walliman, *Estrangement*, pp. 33–34.
22. Rinehart, *The Tyranny of Work*, p. 15.
23. Lillian Breslow Rubin, *Worlds of Pain: Life in the Working-Class Family* (New York: Basic Books, 1976), p. 155.
24. Walliman, *Estrangement*, p. 35.
25. Terkel, *Working*, p. 21.
26. Rinehart, *The Tyranny of Work*, pp. 15–16.
27. Walliman, *Estrangement*, p. 36.
28. Fromm, *Marx's Concept of Man*, p. 53.

29. Terkel, *Working*, p. 165.
30. Fromm, *Marx's Concept of Man*, p. 54.
31. Fromm, *Marx's Concept of Man*, p. 55.
32. Herbert Marcuse, *One-Dimensional Man: Studies in the Ideology of Advanced Industrial Society* (Boston: Beacon Press, 1964), pp. 4–5.
33. Karl Marx, quoted in Fromm, *Marx's Concept of Man*, p. 56.
34. Fromm, *The Sane Society*, p. 142.
35. Marcuse, *One-Dimensional Man*, p. 12.
36. Fromm, *The Sane Society*, p. 144.
37. Edward S. Greenberg, *Workplace Democracy: The Political Effects of Participation* (Ithaca, N.Y.: Cornell University Press, 1986), p. 67.
38. Rinehart, *The Tyranny of Work*, pp. 140–41.
39. Rubin, *Worlds of Pain*, p. 159.
40. Martin Oppenheimer, "The Proletarianization of the Professional," in *Professionalization and Social Change: The Sociological Review Monograph No. 20*, ed. Paul Halmos (Keele, Staffordshire, U.K.: University of Keele, 1973), pp. 213–14.
41. Eliot Freidson, *Professional Powers: A Study of the Institutionalization of Formal Knowledge* (Chicago: University of Chicago Press, 1986), pp. 21–22.
42. Magali Sarfatti Larson, *The Rise of Professionalism: A Sociological Analysis* (Berkeley: University of California Press, 1977), p. 3.
43. Freidson, *Professional Powers*, p. 22.
44. Larson, *The Rise of Professionalism*, p. 246.
45. Ralph L. Blankenship, *Colleagues in Organization: The Social Construction of Professional Work* (New York: John Wiley & Sons, 1977), p. 4.
46. Charles Derber, *Professionals as Workers: Mental Labor in Advanced Capitalism* (Boston: G. K. Hall, 1982), p. 3.
47. *International Encyclopedia of the Social Sciences*, 1968 ed., s.v. "Professions," by Talcott Parsons.
48. Daniel Bell, *The Coming of Post-Industrial Society* (New York: Basic Books, 1973).
49. Ivan Illich, et al., *Disabling Professions* (London: Marion Boyars, 1977), p. 15.
50. Derber, *Professionals as Workers*, p. 5.
51. Larson, *The Rise of Professionalism*, pp. 232–33.
52. Derber, *Professionals as Workers*, pp. 6–7.
53. Rinehart, *The Tyranny of Work*, p. 95.
54. Max Weber, *From Max Weber: Essays in Sociology*, ed. Hans H. Gerth and C. Wright Mills (London: Routledge & Kegan Paul, 1948), pp. 196–98.
55. C. Wright Mills, *White Collar: The American Middle Classes* (New York: Oxford University Press, 1951), p. 114.
56. Oppenheimer, "The Proletarianization of the Professional," p. 214.
57. Magali Sarfatti Larson, "Proletarianization and Educated Labor," *Theory and Society* 9 (January 1980): 163.
58. Ibid., p. 165.
59. Ibid., p. 168.
60. Terkel, *Working*, p. 521.
61. Rinehart, *The Tyranny of Work*, p. 121.
62. Derber, *Professionals as Workers*, p. 8.

63. Amitai Etzioni, ed., *The Semi-Professions and Their Organization: Teachers, Nurses, Social Workers* (New York: Free Press, 1969), pp. vi–vii.

64. Ibid., p. v.

65. Larson, "Proletarianization and Educated Labor," p. 164.

66. Marcia B. Cohen and David Wagner, "Social-Work Professionalism: Reality and Illusion," in *Professionals as Workers*, by Derber, p. 155.

67. Barbara Ehrenreich and John Ehrenreich, "Hospital Workers: A Case Study in the 'New Working Class,'" in *Prognosis Negative: Crisis in the Health Care System*, ed. David Kotelchuck (New York: Vintage, 1976), pp. 191, 199.

68. Christina Maslach, *Burnout: The Cost of Caring* (Englewood Cliffs, N.J.: Prentice-Hall, 1982), p. 73.

69. Ayala M. Pines, "Changing Organizations: Is a Work Environment Without Burnout an Impossible Goal?" in *Job Stress and Burnout: Research, Theory, and Intervention Perspectives*, ed. Whiton Stewart Paine (Beverly Hills: Sage Publications, 1982), p. 192.

70. Maslach, *Burnout*, p. 10.

71. Ibid., p. 57.

72. Ibid., pp. 62–63.

73. Cary Cherniss, *Staff Burnout: Job Stress in the Human Services* (Beverly Hills: Sage Publications, 1980), p. 127.

74. Charles Zastrow, "Understanding and Preventing Burnout," *British Journal of Social Work* 14 (April 1984): 154.

75. Herbert J. Freudenberger, "The Staff Burnout Syndrome in Alternative Institutions," *Psychotherapy: Theory, Research and Practice* 12 (Spring 1975): 73–82.

76. Harvey J. Fischer, "A Psychoanalytic View of Burnout," in *Stress and Burnout in the Human Service Professions*, ed. Barry A. Farber (New York: Pergamon Press, 1983), p. 41.

77. Ibid., p. 45.

78. S. M. Miller and Frank Riessman, *Social Class and Social Policy* (New York: Basic Books, 1968), pp. 271–72.

79. Pines, "Changing Organizations," p. 190.

80. Ayala M. Pines and Elliot Aronson, *Burnout: From Tedium to Personal Growth* (New York: The Free Press, 1981), p. 11.

81. Howard J. Karger, "Burnout as Alienation," *Social Service Review* 55 (June 1981): 272.

82. Karl Marx, "Economic and Philosophical Manuscripts," in *Karl Marx: Early Writings*, ed. and tr. T. B. Bottomore (London: C. A. Watts, 1963), pp. 124–25.

83. Pines and Aronson, *Burnout*, p. 15.

84. Maslach, *Burnout*, p. 3.

85. Cherniss, *Staff Burnout*, p. 16.

86. Brian Baxter, *Alienation and Authenticity: Some Consequences for Organized Work* (London: Tavistock, 1982), p. 71.

87. John R. P. French Jr., and Robert D. Caplan, "Organizational Stress and Individual Strain," in *The Failure of Success*, ed. Alfred J. Marrow (New York: AMACOM, 1972), pp. 30–66.

88. Ibid., p. 51.

89. Ronnie Abush and Jane E. Burkhead, "Job Stress in Midlife Working Women:

Relationships among Personality Type, Job Characteristics, and Job Tension," *Journal of Counseling Psychology* 31 (January 1984): 36–44.

90. Dale G. Shaw, Robert W. Keiper, and Charles E. Flaherty, "Stress Causing Events for Teachers," *Education* 106 (Fall 1985): 72–77.

91. Susan E. Jackson, "Participation in Decision Making as a Strategy for Reducing Job-Related Strain," *Journal of Applied Psychology* 68 (February 1983): 3–19.

92. Rinehart, *The Tyranny of Work*, p. 103.

93. William C. Sze and Barry Ivker, "Stress in Social Workers: The Impact of Setting and Role," *Social Casework* 67 (March 1986): 141–48.

94. Victor Savicki and Eric Cooley, "The Relationship of Work Environment and Client Contact to Burnout in Mental Health Professionals," *Journal of Counseling & Development* 65 (January 1987): 249–52.

95. Diane McDermott, "Professional Burnout and Its Relation to Job Characteristics, Satisfaction, and Control," *Journal of Human Stress* 10 (Summer 1984): 79–85.

96. Nathan M. Smith and Laura F. Nielson, "Burnout: A Survey of Corporate Librarians," *Special Libraries* 75 (July 1984): 224.

97. Heisler, "Worker Alienation," p. 78.

98. Cherniss, *Staff Burnout*, p. 16.

99. Heisler, "Worker Alienation," pp. 74–75.

100. Jerome F. X. Carroll and William L. White, "Theory Building: Integrating Individual and Environmental Factors Within an Ecological Framework," in *Job Stress and Burnout*, ed. Paine, p. 43.

101. William P. Sexton, "Work Humanization in Practice: What Should Business Do?" in *A Matter of Dignity*, ed. Heisler and Houck, p. 134.

102. Heisler, "Worker Alienation," p. 79.

103. Leonard I. Pearlin and Carmi Schooler, "The Structure of Coping," *Journal of Health and Social Behavior* 19 (March 1978): 2–21.

# 3

# Librarianship: An Inevitable Case?

In the last chapter, a case was made for conceptualizing burnout as a manifestation of work alienation. Burnout is both a symptom and a negative consequence of this pervasive condition. The kindling for burnout is laid when individuals, of necessity, sell their labor. Through this transaction they lose control over their work and its products, becoming alienated from their work, from other people, and from themselves. While an economic system in which nearly all individuals must sell their labor is generally considered the broadest and most fundamental structural determinant of work alienation, other structural factors, operating at various levels, are also implicated.

In this chapter we turn to librarianship as a sort of case study in alienation. A number of factors specific to the development of the library profession and to public librarianship in particular have served to increase librarians' susceptibility to professional alienation and burnout. Some of these factors are related to the structure of the profession, for example, the bureaucratic organization of libraries. Others, such as feminization, have affected the position of librarians vis-à-vis the wider social structure. Still others, including elitism and technical orientation, have deepened the estrangement between librarians and the public that they serve.

## THE PRIESTHOOD OF MINERVA

Library history has long paid homage to the founders and philanthropists of the American public library movement as men of high humanitarian ideals, dedicated champions of democracy and liberal reform. More recent analysis suggests that while the early public library did have some positive effects along these lines, such effects often came about despite, rather than through, the intentions of its creators.

The prime movers in the development of American librarianship generated much rhetoric regarding "the common man" but were themselves far from common. As library historian Dee Garrison notes, only a cultured elite would have had sufficient leisure and money to assume the task of establishing public libraries.[1] The class background of such early library leaders as George Ticknor and Edward Everett has been described as "well bred, well educated, well housed, and well heeled."[2] An inventory of the principles to which this patrician class gave allegiance would include the "inevitability of stratification, persistence of natural inequalities, necessity of aristocracy, importance of religion and morality, sanctity of property, unwisdom of majority rule, urgency of constitutionalism, and folly of all attempts at social and economic leveling."[3] Members of this dominant socioeconomic group perceived in the spread of Jacksonian democracy a threat to their accustomed position and way of life. Equally disturbing was the increasing flood of immigration. Many of these foreign newcomers were resistant to the convection of the melting pot; rather than embracing the established institutions and leadership of the New England cultural and economic elite, they were all too often drawn into radical labor movements and the Democratic political machines.

George Ticknor, leader of the Boston Brahmins and a founder of the Boston Public Library, worried that the steadily increasing immigrant population was unfit "to understand our free institutions or to be intrusted with the political power given by universal suffrage," and he strongly advocated education as a "remedy for this influx of ignorance."[4] Public libraries, in Ticknor's view, were essential elements in the educational pharmacopoeia. Library historian Michael Harris observes that Ticknor's elitism and authoritarianism were reflected in his goals for the library: "1) to educate the masses so that they would follow the 'best men' and not demagogues; to 'stabilize the Republic and to keep America from becoming another Carthage'; and 2) to provide access to the world's best books for that elite minority who would someday become leaders of the political, intellectual, and moral affairs of the nation."[5] Many leading lights of the public library movement shared Ticknor's vision of the library as a conservator of social order and the status quo. Charles A. Cutter maintained that libraries, by substituting the cheaper and better amusement of books, would discourage "visits to low resorts."[6] William Frederick Poole believed that the masses, "who had very little of literary and scholarly culture," should be reached through "redeeming" literature.[7] Amid the economic depression and subsequent unemployment of 1893, another librarian confidently stated: "If society cannot provide work for all, the idle—chronic or temporary—are much safer with a book in the library than elsewhere."[8]

Library philanthropists also valued the conservative functions of the institution. One manufacturer supported public education because he had "uniformly found the better educated as a class possessing a higher and better state of morals, more orderly and respectful in their deportment, and more ready to comply with the wholesome and necessary regulations of an establishment."[9] Industrialists and others of great wealth, anxious over the threat of social upheaval posed by urban squalor and the organized reform movements of the late nineteenth century, saw in the library not only an antidote to individual vice but a bulwark against the dangers of growing class consciousness. Libraries were expected to inculcate "good judgement and moral principles" during "these times when heartless demagogues try to array labor against capital, when Georgism, Socialism and Anarchism excite the minds of the masses and threaten to shake the world in its foundations of religion, law and order."[10] Philanthropists such as Andrew Carnegie believed in the virtue and efficacy of self-improvement for the working man. At the same time, they used the philosophy of self-help as a means of ensuring social stability, reasoning that as the poor pulled themselves up by their bootstraps, they would be less likely to jeopardize their hard-won mobility through involvement in radical reform movements.[11]

Trustees of the public library, like its founders and philanthropists, were cast in an elite rather than a common mold. The nineteenth-century library board was almost without exception composed of wealthy, white, Protestant business and professional men.[12] The class background and interests of these early library trustees were often reflected in the characteristics that they sought in the individuals whom they employed in their libraries. It was recommended that the examination of a candidate go back "to his ancestors, to see what of intellectual as well as physical quality he has inherited from them."[13] Lloyd Pearsall Smith, hereditary librarian of the Library Company of Philadelphia, insisted that librarians "should belong to the Brahmin caste."[14] Many of them did. Garrison has compiled a socioeconomic profile of thirty-six librarians who held influential positions in 1885. Of these, 44 percent were descended from prominent New England families of the colonial period.[15]

The trustees and librarians who formed the "public library elite" of the nineteenth century instituted a number of authoritarian measures in keeping with their own aristocratic origins and with the conservative vision of the library's founders and philanthropists. Petty humiliations were frequently imposed over the issue of sanitation. Gently reared librarians tended to value cleanliness highly, while their working-class patrons, whose tenements generally lacked plumbing, understandably considered it more optional. In his role as advisor to the Silas Bronson Library of Waterbury, Connecticut, Poole decreed: "Ample arrangements having been made for washing, the attendants are instructed to deliver no periodical or book into unclean hands."[16]

An incident at the Chicago Public Library in the 1880s illustrates just how sincere one library was in its commitment to serving the common man. A "regular clientele of unwashed devotees of the daily newspapers" was presenting an "offense to the olfactory senses" of librarians and more sweet-smelling patrons. Improved ventilation was only partially successful in reducing the nuisance, as was assignment of a police officer to the reading room. When the move to new quarters in 1886 required the elimination of certain services to allow for the expansion of others, a happy resolution to the problem of the unwashed undesirables was found: current American newspapers were no longer made available to the public.[17]

Libraries not infrequently enlisted the support of police and other formal public authorities in their quest for moral control over their patrons. In 1882, the city council of Bridgeport, Connecticut, levied stiff fines not only for the destruction of library property but for disorderly conduct on library premises. In addition, a city policeman was periodically detailed to the library to verify borrowers' references, to collect fines, and, at the librarian's request, to supervise users of the reading room.[18] The New York Public Library's (NYPL) harsh treatment of a schoolboy book thief in 1897 generated much public sympathy for the culprit and animosity toward the library. The incident also resulted in NYPL's hiring an attendant to patrol the reading rooms and keep readers under surveillance.[19] Prominent librarian Justin Winsor summed up the hard line taken by many of his colleagues toward violators: "[Boston's] immunity from loss comes from a rigid system of following up delinquents, which we have been practising for twenty-five years, for our gain and for the moral advantage of our citizens."[20]

The elitism and authoritarianism of the early library are perhaps most apparent in the censorship that it imposed on the reading matter of the public. In their zeal to uplift and improve the working class, librarians and library boards were determined to provide only those books they considered uplifting and improving. Library historian Rosemary Ruhig DuMont notes that reading was intended to instill ideals in the poor: "Books were to provide moral and mental stimuli by revealing to them the courtesy, polite manners, and social customs of the modest American family."[21] Titles containing references to nudity or condoning behavior that was not properly conventional by Victorian standards were generally excluded.[22] Children were the beneficiaries of especially vigilant censorship. Questionable books, if not banned outright, were kept behind desks, in locked cases, or on open shelves with coded labels on their spines. Classic works such as the *Decameron* were often purchased in bowdlerized editions. The novels of Theodore Dreiser were routinely banned, as was *Madame Bovary*. Fiction itself was considered highly suspect; debate raged for decades in library literature as to whether to allow it shelf space under any circumstances. "The Censor," which appeared in *Library Journal* in 1891, betokens a subtler but none the less real form of librarian coercion:

> She's a priestess of Minerva
>   With a scorn of lighter things;
> And no idle smile can swerve her,
>   For she guards the Pierian springs.
> And she draws the sparkling waters
>   For the learned and the weak,
> Giving maidens "Beauty's Daughters,"
>   And professors crabbed Greek.
>
> If I ask for Herbert Spencer,
>   Or for Plato or Carlyle,
> I can catch the pretty censor
>   In a faint approving smile;
> But at Anna Karenina,
>   Or the gay *contes* of France,
> She wears a cold demeanor
>   And a blushing, downcast glance.[23]

The authoritarianism of the early public library was no harsher than that practiced in the schools, offices, and factories of the period. It was largely self-defeating, however, given the voluntary nature of library use. The cold, inflexible, and coercive atmosphere of the library caused people to question its egalitarian stance and repelled the very working-class clientele it set out to attract. A 1908 exhortation to make libraries more welcoming to industrial workers bears a striking resemblance to more contemporary expressions of concern over the library's unserved clienteles: "Industrial workers have hitherto, on the whole, kept out of public libraries because of a suspicion—perhaps not entirely without foundation—that they are not wanted there. . . . It has taken a generation of cold exclusiveness to generate this idea."[24] Most early librarians were well-intentioned, even dedicated pubic servants; the institutional policies that they enforced, however, were typically designed not to enhance library users' freedom and autonomous development but to support a status quo that flourished through a class system of dominance and dependence. In the consciously elitist nature of the early library and in its orientation toward its users as means to an end—in this case, social stasis—rather than as valid ends in themselves, a century-long dynamic of misunderstanding, distrust, and generalized estrangement was set in train.

## THE FETISHISM OF TECHNIQUE

With the approach of the new century, librarians' concern over philosophical matters was supplanted by a growing professional attention to the technical and economic aspects of library service. The modernistic ideal of the library as "a good machine, with every belt and cog well adjusted, with all its bearings well oiled"[25] was pursued with no less fervor than was the previous mission to preserve social order. Librarians' emerging fascination with numbers is evident in the annual reports of the day, which concentrated much attention on circulation figures and little on the qualitative aspects of library programs.[26] Professional literature abounded with debate and advice on the best methods for improving the efficiency of library techniques. In 1896 alone, the pages of *Public Libraries* were host to articles on accessioning books, author cards, binding, binding slips, book card trays, book labels, book plates, call numbers, capitalization, card pockets, cataloging and classification, catalogs, catalog cards, catalog cases, chair design, charging systems, colored cards, cost of cataloging (per thousand cards), cumulative indexes, and cutting book leaves. The proliferation of such topics continued through the alphabet.

The major prophet of this new technical pragmatism was Melvil Dewey—or Dui, as he spelled it to make the most efficient use of even so unrationed a resource as letters. Best known for his decimal classification, Dewey tirelessly urged the saving of time in all areas of library operations. In his writing and addresses, Dewey promoted the use of such labor-saving devices as typewriters, duplicators, and dictaphones and gave lavish advice on the standardization and selection of cards, files, boxes, bells, rulers, stationery, shelves, and fountain pens.[27] In an 1886 issue of his own quarterly magazine, *Library Notes*, Dewey published a nine-page article detailing the optimal size and form of library handwriting.[28] It is Dewey who coined the thrifty motto of the American Library Association (ALA), "The best reading for the largest number at the least cost."[29] He also promoted an efficiency-motivated interlibrary cooperation: "We have learned from the industrial captains that work can be done cheaper and better if it is concentrated; if we are to take our part in this great world movement we must cooperate, we must work with our associates."[30] Impatient with the "unsympathetic fossils" who still presided in many libraries, Dewey railed against "'good form' which assumes that time and money are of no account."[31]

Dewey had an enthusiastic follwing among young librarians, but he did encounter some resistance. William Frederick Poole, during his tenure as president of the ALA, delivered a philosophical statement in which the gap between the older cohort of gentleman scholars and Dewey's new generation of library technicians is quite evident:

Some librarians surround themselves with short-hand writers and much routine. Every emergency is provided for by a rule or contrivance, and every sort of business transaction, by an armory of hand-stamps. Other librarians take delight in doing work in the simplest way; in meeting emergencies as they arise; in reducing each business operation to its lowest terms, and in turning over to subordinates work they can do well. Such librarians are not swamped in an ocean of detail; they write their own letters, are delightful correspondents, and have time to attend to the higher and bibliographical wants of their libraries.[32]

Despite such gentle caveats, the reduction of librarianship to a mechanical art continued apace. Carolyn Hewins, first woman vice president of the ALA, wrote in 1891 of the qualifications expected of applicants to the New York State Library School at Albany. "Habits of system and order" figured so high on the list that "the most distinguished librarian in the country has always asked . . . concerning a new applicant, 'Does she keep her bureau drawers in order?' "[33] By 1917, a manual on the organization of small libraries was informing its readers: "An economy of time that is growing in favor among trained librarians is disuse of capitals and punctuation marks wherever clearness of meaning is not thereby sacrificed."[34]

The shift in focus from qualitative to quantitative matters can be partly explained in pragmatic terms; burgeoning collections were quickly rendering the cataloging and classification schemes of many early-established libraries inadequate. Beyond this fact, however, was the widespread admiration for scientific objectivity and for business enterprise, with their aura of efficiency, modernity, and technocratic power. Librarians, in their quest for professional status, often tried to model their institutions after profit-making concerns. Such consuming interested in technical details may also represent a retreat from broader social issues in response to the library's failure to meet the goals set down by its founders.

The enduring technical orientation of the library profession has worked to alienate librarians from the public no less than have the library's traditional elitism and authoritarianism. Psychologist Murray Levine argues that a critical factor in professional alienation is the over-reliance on professional method: "Paradoxically, it is our strength which is our weakness, for the methods and concepts by which we lay claim to a special relationship to other people are precisely that which stands between ourselves and others, and between ourselves and the human phenomena which intrigued us into our field of interst in the first place."[35] In the course of professional practice, notes Levine, the emphasis too often shifts from concern for the client to checking and correcting artifacts of method.[36] Concentration on professional techniques may enhance the sense of professional identity, but, at the same time, it has distanced librarians from library users, making it more difficult to perceive and respond to their needs. Such a focus also serves to alienate librarians from the work process itself, as the techniques become reified and assume an authority of their own, reducing both the need and the opportunity for innovation and creative decision making. Over-reliance on professional methods and techniques alienates librarians from their own interests as well, causing them to lose touch with the concerns which brought them to choose the profession for their life's work.

## THE SCIENTIFICALLY MANAGED LIBRARY

Professional fascination with quantitative and mechanistic reductionism soon spread from its application to technical and economic aspects of library service to the operation of the library as a whole. As early as 1905, librarians were advised that "to make public libraries a success in the widest sense they must be operated by those methods which make a business successful."[37] Foremost among these methods were scientific management and bureaucratic organization.

Introduced originally to increase productivity in industry, scientific management enjoyed a wide popularity during the early years of this century, its principles soon being extended to public administration. At the heart of scientific management is "the establishment of many rules, laws, and formulae which replace the judgment of the individual workman and which can be effectively used only after having been systematically recorded, indexed, etc."[38] This was heady stuff to a profession already dazzled by method and technique. Frederick Winslow Taylor, the movement's founder, believed that "the tendency of the average man (in all walks of life) is toward working at a slow, easy gait, and that it is only after a good deal of thought and observation on his part or as a result of example, conscience, or external pressure that he takes a more rapid pace."[39] A basic premise of scientific management is that prosperity can be attained only when individuals have reached their highest state of efficiency—their "largest daily output"—and that it is the responsibility of administrators to ensure that this happy state of affairs comes about.[40]

Such calculation was not new to librarianship. In 1902, nine years before Taylor's *Principles of Scientific Management* was published, Dewey wrote on the importance of executive ability to the librarian:

[It is the] power to organize and delegate work, to marshall and use four m's which produce results: i.e. materials, machinery (tools, labor-saving devices), methods, men. Without this [you] can get only maximum wages for [the] individual. With it you get pay for what others do. This is unjust no more than to take pay for utilizing forces of nature, horses or mere labor.[41]

Anticipating the time-and-motion studies that were to become fundamental to Taylorism, Dewey urged librarians to "keep a watch or clock hanging before you."[42]

In addition to the innate mechanistic appeal of scientific management and Dewey's impassioned advocacy of it, librarians were drawn to the movement because of its potential as a conservative, stabilizing force. Garrison remarks that scientific management represented a restatement of traditional religious values, including exhortations to hard work, self-denial, control of sensuality, and passive submission to legitimate authority.[43]

By the 1920s, scientific management had become integral to the practice of librarianship. A textbook published by the ALA in 1928 emphasizes the new role of the librarian as a manager:

> We have had generations of librarians who were collectors of books, bibliographers, classifiers, catalogers, and scholars. The urge today, following the tendency of the times, is to emphasize the organization and administration of book service. The librarian is the executive officer of the library. . . . He should be a good executive and administrator, able to organize work effectively, to formulate plans and policies, to make decisions, and to direct the work of others.[44]

As public libraries increased in size and complexity, their internal organization became commensurately more bureaucratic. Librarians generally accepted as axiomatic that "effective administrative organization is a hierarchy."[45] This progressive bureaucratization of libraries served to reinforce the entrenchment of scientific management. Sharing the goal of maximizing efficiency through task specialization, bureaucracy and scientific management have a natural affinity. In addition, the hierarchical "chain of command" basic to bureaucratic structure corrected a weakness of early Taylorism—the overlapping authority resulting from workers' being responsible to more than one supervisor.[46]

Despite the moderating effects of more recent trends in personnel management, particularly the human relations and quality-of-worklife movements, the philosophy and methods of scientific management are far from defunct. They continue to influence management theory and styles in terms of: 1) the central emphasis on efficiency; 2) the concept of task specialization; 3) the use of such extrinsic rewards as salary and status to motivate workers; and 4) a structured and systematic form of organizational control.[47] A widely read handbook on scientific management for libraries, published in 1966, offered much advice to the librarian-manager. One suggestion was to group employees' desks in such a way as to discourage conversation.[48] In their 1982 revised edition, the authors continued to recommend the application of motion economy to routine library tasks: "The hands should not both be idle at the same time during a cycle. Motions of the arms should be made in opposite and symmetrical directions. Holds and delays should be minimized because they are not productive."[49] Diagrammatic evidence of the hierarchal form of authority still prevalent in most libraries of any size is provided by the flow charts featured in nearly every library administration textbook.

Scientific management, together with the bureaucratic structure of libraries and the profession's devotion to technical proficiency, has resulted in a mechanistic institution with a traditionally inward-looking, means-centered orientation. Quantitative management methods are typically conservative in their effects. Directed toward improving the means by which current programs and services are provided—often involving increasingly sophisticated technology—scientific management is rarely receptive to a renegotiation of ends. It has been estimated, for example, that as many as 70 to 90 percent of all library tasks consist of repetitive, mechanical routines.[50] For the scientific manager, this finding is positive, calling for the quantitative analysis of such tasks, their further routinization in the interests of greater efficiency, and possibly the introduction of new staffing ratios. The scientific manager is less likely to act on a related finding—that where library service is organized as a community "outreach" activity, the professional component of librarians' work nearly doubles.[51]

The autocratic nature of traditional library management is reflected in the advice of prominent library educator Herbert S. White:

We must provide an environment in which individuals can reconcile their personal objectives (diverse as these are) to organizational objectives. Most subordinates are willing to meet us more than halfway, because they accept the premise that in order to be paid they and their co-workers ought to do something productive.[52]

The legacy of scientific management has been the stifling of professional autonomy for librarians and the stagnation of their institutions. While scientific management can accommodate a certain amount of input from the ranks, this accommodation is compromised by both the authority hierarchy and the limited range of officially sanctioned organizational objectives. The emphasis on procedural regularity has decreased librarians' scope for professional judgment and innovation while at the same time often reducing interactions between librarians and library users to brief, mechanized "production units." (It is an unwritten policy at some large libraries that librarians devote no more than three minutes to each reference request.) The overall effect of such a management system can be "to make the librarian feel that some vast, mechanistic 'open prison' has been built around him which is invincible *on its own terms*, and in which he is 'free' to make only a limited range and kind of choice."[53]

## WOMEN'S WORK AND MALE AUTHORITY

In the earliest days of the American public library movement, the notion of hiring women as librarians was rejected as an impropriety. Charles Folsom, librarian of the Boston Athenaeum, declared that the presence of women in a library containing examples of "the corrupter portions of the polite literature" would cause "frequent embarrassment to modest men."[54] Male blushes were soon brought under control, however, in the face of economic imperatives. By the late nineteenth century, the growth of public libraries was rapidly outstripping their support from public and philanthropic sources. Because of the labor-intensive nature of library work, an escalating need developed for employees who were both well educated and willing to accept low salaries. For those who had the responsibility of balancing library budgets, it was a happy coincidence that the first waves of college-educated women were beginning to enter the labor market.

In Victorian society, which revered the gentle and genteel ideal of the "true woman," few paid employment opportunities existed for female college graduates. This limitation on career options, together with the typically low pay offered by libraries, served to bring more women than men into librarianship during the last quarter of the nineteenth century. The first woman librarian is believed to have been hired by William Poole at the Boston Athenaeum in 1857.[55] By 1910, nearly 80 percent of library workers were women.[56]

Like its sister professions, teaching, nursing, and social work, librarianship was considered particularly suited to feminine talents and sensibilities. Nurturing the young, tending the sick—though not in the authoritative role of physician—and dispensing cheer and charity to the poor were deemed appropriate extensions of woman's primarily domestic role. Librarianship, with its emphasis on moral and cultural uplift, fit comfortably within the popular Victorian concept of the "women's sphere." In his address to British and American librarians at the 1877 conference in London, Justin Winsor praised the special qualities that women brought to library work:

In American libraries we set a high value on women's work. They soften our atomosphere, they lighten our labor, they are equal to our work, and for the money they cost—if we must gauge such labor by such rules—they are infinitely better than equivalent salaries will produce of the other sex.[57]

In 1894, Amherst College librarian William I. Fletcher wrote that "librarianship affords a fine field for woman's work," especially for the college-educated. "In the various movements for making libraries more useful and popular, women have been pioneers; their readier sympathies qualify them for inspiring and guiding young readers, and advancing the 'missionary' features of public-library work."[58]

As might be expected, the library's children's room was viewed as an especially suitable workplace for women. It was, in fact, considered inappropriate for male librarians to work directly with children. Between 1895 and 1910, when many large public libraries created specialized positions for children's librarians, no attempts were made to recruit men.[59] Feminine gentleness was not only considered essential for guiding tender young minds through the shoals of literature but thought to have a civilizing effect on potentially rowdy adolescents. At the International Library Conference of 1897, Alderman H. Rawson, of Manchester, asserted that women's "services in the reading-rooms set apart for boys are especially valuable, exercising a restraining influence over the lads, and conducing to quietness, order, and decorum."[60]

Women were also considered particularly well suited to such technical library tasks as indexing and cataloging. Of the 100 institutions surveyed by Salome Cutler Fairchild in her 1904 study of women in American libraries, most preferred to hire women for cataloging positions because of their "greater conscientiousness, patience and accuracy in details."[61] Frequent reference was made to the "infinite capacity for taking pains . . . constantly to be found in women."[62] Dewey, in his unflagging pursuit of technical proficiency, complimented the woman librarian for her "deft fingers," which "do many things with a neatness and despatch seldom equalled by her brothers."[63] Another reason for relegating routine, repetitive tasks to female library workers is less flattering—women were believed to have a higher boredom threshold than men. "The enthusiasm a woman usually puts into her work is a great leaven and tends to lift the most monotonous task out of the commonplace."[64]

During the Progressive era, then, women were welcomed into the profession with open arms. Dewey even carried out "recruiting raids" on college women heading for careers in education, urging them to consider the advantages of librarianship. Library work was less physically taxing, he argued, and librarians were not subject to the "nervous strain and the wear and tear of the classroom."[65] While librarianship did represent a true career opportunity for educated women in the late nineteenth century it was not, however, an unlimited opportunity. Women librarians were typically paid at half the rate of their male colleagues and often received even less than the notoriously underpaid urban schoolteacher.[66] One woman librarian remarked that the ability to live on two meals a day was a necessary qualification for the job.[67]

Library literature of the period contains plentiful references to the advancement opportunities enjoyed by American women librarians. And it is true that the career situation on this side of the Atlantic was less restricted than that described by British Museum librarian John MacFarlane in 1898: "There is yet no serious question—such is male arrogance—of employing women in the more scholarly libraries, though when the British Museum took over the Tapling collection of postage stamps, a lady was engaged to assist in the delicate work of arranging and cataloging them."[68] Still, while women dominated the field numerically, men held most positions of authority. Library historian Barbara Brand remarks that the pattern, established in teaching, of underpaying women and excluding them from influential positions transferred directly to librarianship.[69] In her turn-of-the-century survey, Fairchild found that in nineteen out of twenty-one large public libraries, the head librarians were men. Men were also in charge of all six reference and three government libraries surveyed. Of the twenty-four coeducational academic libraries in the study, twenty were administered by men, as were the five proprietary and four subscription libraries.[70] This "masculinization at the top" was matched by a "territorial segregation," which found men disproportionately represented in those areas considered most prestigious and professional, such as academic librarianship.[71]

Justifications abounded for economically exploiting women librarians and for fixing strict limits on their autonomy and authority. In an ironic twist, many of these justifications were based on those same feminine qualities so extolled as fitting the gentler sex for the profession in the first place. In the words of a (male) library trustee:

My reason for preferring a man for the head of a library in a large city is not based on what may be called the library *per se*. It is connected with the business side of the librarian's position. Unfortunately women are hedged about with rules of decorum and courtesy which somewhat interfere with their usefulness in many relations in a municipal or a business community.[72]

In common with all members of their sex, women librarians were generally assumed to lack "a head for business." It was argued that women (appropriately) shun rather than court responsibility, that they are not in touch with the world of affairs, that they are temperamental, inflexible, unpunctual, incapable of managing a "mixed" staff, subject to petty jealousies, and more easily demoralized over trifles.[73] Dewey, while protesting with some justice that he did not personally discriminate against women in his business and professional life, wrote as an apologist for those who did. The "consideration which she exacts and deserves on account of her sex" makes the woman librarian less versatile than a man, Dewey contended. "There are many uses for which a stout corduroy is really worth more than the finest silk."[74]

The widespread preference of governing boards for male library administrators, coupled with a growing concern over the effect feminization might have on librarianship's image and prestige, led to an increasing call for inducting more men into the profession. In the wake of the librarian shortage occasioned by World War II, both the armed services and various library associations mounted recruitment campaigns emphasizing the financial rewards of administrative library work and the preference that men received in advancing to such positions.[75] To a certain extent, these campaigns were successful. Between 1940 and 1950, the number of male librarians nearly doubled and did so again between 1950 and 1960.[76] Librarianship remains a sex-typed profession, however. Eighty-seven percent of librarians are women.[77] The recruitment campaigns also succeeded in exacerbating sex segregation within the profession, "the impact of the sudden surge of men into librarianship" being to intensify "the existing trend of placing men in top administrative posts."[78] This pattern continues as well. A 1981 survey of public libraries serving populations of 100,000 or more in the United States and Canada found that two-thirds of them have male directors.[79]

While dissenting opinions have been forcibly and eloquently expressed over the years in professional forums and in library literature, the feminization of librarianship continues to be held responsible for thwarting professional development and preventing public recognition. Library historian Dee Garrison, while documenting the discrimination directed toward women librarians during the Progressive period, considers that their mere presence in such numbers produced negative effects. She cites the preponderance of female students, "who most likely lacked scholarly ambitions or preparation; who had no lifelong vocational commitment; and whose attitudes toward feminine sex roles led [them] to accept, and expect, administrative controls, low autonomy, and subordination to clerical, routine tasks," as a factor in the concentration on mechanical routines by library schools.[80] Garrison argues that the feminization of library work was a major cause of three professional deficiencies: 1) the lack of a professional sense of commitment to work; 2) an orientation toward service rather than leadership; and 3) an unclear concept of professional rights and responsibilities.[81]

Phyllis Dain, also a library historian, agrees that librarianship's lack of professional status is connected to the feminization of the field, but in subtler ways:

The connection that culture came to have with women and the anti-intellectualism that tinged bookishness with effeminacy must also have figured in the attitude toward librarians in a society that so highly valued masculine attitudes and striving. Furthermore, no matter how much lip service was paid to the adage "knowledge is power," people who organized and made knowledge available on a nonprofit and voluntary, nonfee basis rather than creating and selling it, would not be generally conceived as powerful.[82]

Dain's argument can be taken a step further: women are viewed not only as relatively powerless in our society but as weaker than men physically, intellectually, economically. To the extent that librarianship is associated with women—and it remains closely associated, indeed, as is evident in the persistent stereotype of the librarian as a repressed and compulsively orderly female—it, too, is considered powerless and is devalued accordingly. The numerical predominance of women has not compromised the professional integrity of librarianship; rather, traditional and pervasive sexist attitudes have contributed to a continued societal undervaluing of the profession. It is reasonable to assume that this undervaluing has been a major factor in the public's reluctance to accord librarianship full professional status and thus in the circumscription of the professional autonomy of librarians.

Equally significant in contributing to librarians' lack of autonomy and subsequent susceptibility to work alienation is the traditional sex segregation within the profession. Garrison asserts that most early women librarians accepted the "male-structured" view of women as inherently limited in the working world. "Within librarianship and other feminized occupations, compliance with sex roles prevented women from assuming such autonomy."[83] In this assertion, Garrison echoes the ideas of Simpson and Simpson in their 1969 study on women and bureaucracy, a study which posited that women are predisposed to compliance and that such compliance works to reinforce bureaucratic authoritarianism.[84] This victim-blaming approach seems to have little explanatory validity, however, given the evidence that when women librarians were allowed some autonomy, they showed no tendency to abdicate their responsibility. Children's librarianship, for example, long the exclusive domain of woman librarians, "was unusual among contemporary library specialties in creating a knowledge base beyond the techniques of the work."[85] If women librarians have participated in their own exploitation, they have done so as the result of socialization directly aimed at their social control. The notion that men have a natural right to authority over women and the acceptance of this notion by the public, by governing boards, and by many male librarians have been enduringly salient factors in susppressing the professional autonomy of the majority of librarians.

## PROFESSIONALISM AND THE BARRIER OF BUREAUCRACY

Sinced the first ALA conference in 1876, professionalism has been a serious concern of librarians. The goal of an organized and unified profession was a primary motivation of Dewey and his followers in their campaign to standardize and mechanize librarianship. The formalization of library education represented another step toward professionalization. But the public remained hard to convince. A prominent academic librarian, writing in 1894, found the progress up to that point perceptible but far from impressive: "Librarianship is not one of the recognized, learned professions; in fact it is but just beginning to be acknowledged as something more than a function, for the exercise of which any fairly educated or even ordinarily intelligent person is quite competent."[86]

From 1890 on, increasing numbers of librarians became concerned that the extreme technical-clerical orientation of library schools was hampering professional development.[87] The Williamson report's scathing indictment of library education in 1923 confirmed their fears. Based on his study of all fifteen American library schools then in existence, Williamson concluded that "no school has ever attempted or is now prepared to disregard what has been done in the past and make a thorough, scientific analysis of what training for professional library work should be and build its curriculum upon its findings, instead of following tradition and imitating others."[88]

Another blow to the profession's self-esteem was delivered in 1961 upon publication of William Goode's evaluation of librarianship as an occupation lacking and unlikely to accede to full professional status.[89] Librarianship, Goode contends, has failed to develop a general body of scientific knowledge pertaining to its occupational tasks. Nor does the public believe librarianship to have such a knowledge base. Because the knowledge base is undeveloped, librarians tend to assume administrative roles earlier than individuals in other careers, thus leading to an occupational hierarchy in which the more senior members are concerned with management rather than with generating new professional knowledge. Without a firm knowledge base and its recognition by the public, librarianship's claim to professional expertise and autonomy is seriously compromised. Basing his arguments largely on the Code of Ethics adopted by the ALA in 1938, Goode concludes that, unlike doctors and lawyers, librarians have little power over their clients. Librarians do not dictate to or prescribe for their clients; they serve them by helping to fulfill their stated needs and wants: "The librarian is a gatekeeper who can exclude almost no one; a guardian who can protect primarily against vandals and thieves; a stockroom custodian who must hand over any of his stock even if he is sure the person really wants or needs something else."[90]

In response to Goode's criticisms and to similar conclusions reached by other investigators librarianship increasingly focused its attention on the issues surrounding professionalization.[91] Library school curricula were reassessed. The ALA adopted a somewhat stronger and more professionally oriented ethics code in 1975.[92] In the cause of professionalism, attempts were made to identify and develop librarianship's elusive knowledge base.[93] Acceptance of the traditional professional paradigm was not universal, however. Reservations regarding both the validity of Goode's conclusions and their relevance to librarianship have been expressed. In his study on the professionalization of librarianship, Michael Winter remarks that Goode's allegation that librarians do not contribute to the knowledge base "should not be held against any occupation, for it is usually teachers and scholars who carry out these functions and not practitioners." Further, he cites studies demonstrating a relatively high degree of contribution to the research literature by working librarians.[94] Reference librarian Bonnie Nelson argues that the two elements central to Goode's professional model—monopoly over a knowledge base and authority over the client—are inappropriate goals for librarianship.

> In fact, the librarian is dedicated to making available to the lay public that knowledge which the professional is anxious to control. The professional keeps his client in a subservient position. The librarian respects his client by collecting information, making it available, and instructing the client in how to locate it; the client is assumed to have the intelligence to know what to do with it.[95]

Librarians, Nelson contends, should stop chasing the "chimera of professionalism." Canadian librarian William Birdsall concurs. Allowing that such typically professional characteristics as advanced degree programs, ethical codes, and professional associations can be a means toward more effective service, he voices the concern that "librarians too often see these as ends in themselves, forgetting that they do not inherently guarantee better service or greater professionalism."[96] Citing Haug and Sussman's influential study of public opinion and professionalism, Birdsall asserts that a critical factor in improving the image and prestige of an emerging profession is the successful experience of clients in utilizing its services. It is the client, then, who ultimately defines the professional, not the general public.[97] Therefore, Birdsall continues, librarians would tread a surer route to professionalism by working to strengthen the client-librarian relationship.

Both the classic professional paradigm, with its emphasis on control, and the newer client-centered approach advocated by Nelson and Birdsall are difficult if not impossible to realize within a bureaucratic structure. Libraries are bureaucracies. Academic and corporate libraries, unless they are very small, are bureaucracies within bureaucracies. The history of public library development is also the history of its bureaucratization. The goals of library bureaucracies differ little from those of others:

The emphasis in most organizations, including libraries, is to make tasks routine, reduce uncertainty, increase predictability, and centralize authority. . . . The elements of bureaucracy emerge from the library's attempt to ensure its efficiency and its competency and from its attempt to minimize the impact of outside influences.[98]

Bureaucratization and professionalism have been said to bear an inverse relationship to each other.[99] This is due to the inevitable conflict between bureaucratic authority, which is based upon official position and requires subordination to its directives, and professional authority, which is rooted in professional expertise and requires autonomy. Supervision, "the telling of people what to do and the overseeing that they do it," may be more excessive in libraries than in other professional organizations.[100] The hierarchical authority structure of libraries strictly limits the discretionary sphere of even veteran librarians. If a librarian perceives the need to change the most minor procedure, he or she must generally appeal to the next link in the "chain of command," and since this individual's greater authority is combined with a greater vested interest in the status quo, the impetus for innovation may be quite limited. Mary Lee Bundy suggests that those who hold authority positions within library bureaucracies tend to be "power holding" rather than "power striving"; that is, they seek to retain the authority they have rather than to augment it through some analogue of corporate expansion. This orientation, according to Bundy, may result in less exploitation of workers but also in greater suppression of their autonomy.[101]

The bureaucratic structure of libraries compromises librarians' professional autonomy and, consequently, the client-librarian relationship in a number of ways. Librarians' professional goals, which generally involve improving quality of service, must ordinarily be subordinated to organizational goals, which emphasize efficiency and stability. Even when a proposed innovation requires no diversion of resources beyond the librarian's own time (and control over one's own time is the hallmark of a professional), permission must be sought and will rarely be granted if the change is perceived to conflict with bureaucratic procedures. Thus, librarians may be unable to arrange their work schedules to enable them to attend community meetings, may be discouraged from participating in social activism, may find roadblocks thrown up when they attempt liaisons with other social service workers, or may be informed that current services are adequate. Conflict between professional and organizational goals, in addition to limiting autonomy and reducing service to users, contributes to librarian role strains.

As with corporate and other public bureaucracies, libraries exert a proletarianizing effect on their professional employees. Participation in policy decisions is generally low. Workloads and work hours are only minimally negotiable. The work environment of librarians often resembles the factory floor more closely than it does the professional suite. While those in top administrative positions will have private offices, other professional personnel—in both technical and public services—have little space or privacy in which to work. Reference desks, generally placed to maximize their visibility, rarely have even a screen to suggest the confidentiality of a professional consultation. With the exception of the staff lounge, librarians typically have no nonpublic space in which to think, plan, read, or relax. Libraries often impose an extensive division of labor on professional as well as clerical employees: "The work of the librarian is most often described in terms of a librarian-client relationship, a one-to-one relationship. Yet much of the work performed in libraries is divided into specialized tasks and is conducted outside the framework of the client relationship."[102] Task routinization and specialization can reduce librarian autonomy to minor decisions regarding technique, and often these are fully prescribed as well. The deskilling of librarians' expertise because of rigid task specialization renders them less versatile contenders in the labor market and thus more dependent on their present employment. It also prevents librarians from adopting a holistic approach to clients' needs; one reference request may necessitate the client's referral to several other librarians for computer searching or advice on adult education. Client-librarian relationships can only be fragmentary under such circumstances. Bureaucratization may also exert a more generalized adverse effect on this relationship. Depersonalization, a key element of the burnout syndrome, has been found to be more prevalent among librarians working in large—and presumably highly bureaucratized—libraries, than in small ones.[103]

Librarians' opportunities for professional advancement are abridged by the library bureaucracy as well. A major criticism Goode leveled at librarianship concerns the identification of professional success and career advancement with assumption of administrative roles. He ascribed this tendency to the lack of a professional knowledge base. Simpson and Simpson assert that this tendency is characteristic of the semi-professions. While the eminent scholar or brilliant surgeon may be more esteemed than the university dean or hospital administrator, to be a successful semi-professional is generally to ascend to a management position. "Lacking a genuinely professional base for recognition, semi-professional organizations create a proliferation of hierarchical levels which provide status badges."[104] It seems specious, however, to hold the profession's alleged lack of a knowledge base responsible for its bureaucratic organization and for its members' ambitions to rise in the hierarchy. A more likely explanation lies in the nature of bureaucratic organization itself, which concentrates power, remuneration, and prestige at the top of the pyramid. Bureaucracies do not reward professional competence—or brilliance—at the lower levels, even with increased autonomy. The only route to advancement is up through the hierarchy itself: "Many librarians have recognized their professional impotency and have cast off the librarian's mantle and assumed that of administrator."[105]

Bureaucratic discouragement of professionalism, with its components of suppressed autonomy, role strains, and proletarianization, is a potent inducer of work alienation. The bureaucratic structure of libraries has also fostered and enhanced the alienating effects of all the other developmental factors considered thus far.

## AMBIGUITY AND ALIENATION: A PROFESSION WITHOUT A PURPOSE

Revisionist historian Michael Harris argues not only that the original (conservative) purpose of the public library has been obscured by the platitudes of the day and by subsequent uncritical accounts but that the entire history of the institution has been characterized by a "recurring cycle of fitful and outer-directed . . . crusades," temporarily embraced by a profession lacking a clear purpose of its own.[106] Harris considers the central theme in the development of American librarianship to be librarians' enduring desire for admission to the "professional pantheon," that elite nucleus of vocations whose members are accorded great power and prestige in American society. This quest for occupational status has caused the profession to embark on a series of crusades in response to cues from the government, church, and press. All of these reactive crusades were undertaken against perceived threats to American values and were aimed toward maintaining social stasis. In the nineteenth century, librarians crusaded against immoral fiction and the impact of low culture, later striving to "Americanize" the successive waves of immigrants. Libraries became "agencies of patriotic publicity" during World

War I, librarians zealously censoring pro-German materials and promoting the reading of Allied works. In the next war, public libraries were called upon to contribute to the preservation of democracy by providing information impartially and adopting a stance of absolute neutrality. Despite often impassioned professional rhetoric, however, none of these externally imposed missions ever received librarians' wholehearted commitment. Lacking an internally generated purpose for the public library, the profession reverted repeatedly "to a mindless focus on technical and bureaucratic matters" once each perceived threat receded.[107]

The widespread reexamination of social values and institutions during the 1960s served to focus increasing attention on the role of the public library. It became clear that with the evaporation of the social forces that had shaped the early institution, the library lacked a purpose to justify its social mandate. As one librarian remarked at the time: "We have inherited a situation in which libraries of various kinds have 'arrived' out of historical accident to a large extent, the forces or circumstances which gave them both birth and *raison d'être* having to a greater or lesser extent passed away, leaving them largely lacking in sense of purpose or clear direction."[108]

The past two decades have been witness to a continuing professional debate over what the role of the public library should be in light of shifting demographic patterns, increased social investment in technology, an uncertain economy, and other developments. The "Mission Statement for Public Libraries," published by the ALA in 1979, recommends a broad and multiple role for public librarians, charging them with the responsibility to serve the total community, to continue to act as popularizers of the human record, to cooperate with other information professionals, and to provide leadership to all libraries "in their response to today's new social needs."[109] Lawrence White, an economist rather than a librarian, rejects broad social and educational roles for the library as "myth." He favors an "information utility" model, similar to the telephone service, which would focus almost exclusively on the lending of books for fees.[110] Douglas Zweizig, responding to the 1983 report on American education, *A Nation at Risk*, argues for expanding the library's educational role.[111] Others envision the public library as an agency of social change, with a special responsibility to the disfranchised.[112]

While there is no shortage of opinion on what the library's role should be, there is a distinct lack of consensus. In a 1984 study, 612 articles appearing in one regional and three national library periodicals over the preceding three years were analyzed to determine whether a unified, explicit description of the purpose and role of the public library was recorded in the professional periodical literature. The investigators found few articles dealing with the subject and even fewer that did so in a sustained, significant manner. The literature was found to be highly fragmented and to present conflicting perceptions of an appropriate role concept for the public library. Further, many authors confused programs and services (means) with roles and purposes (ends). The investigators concluded that the professional literature on the public library's role—or the lack of it—may actively contribute to public librarians' having "a strong sense of ambiguity on the subject . . . leading to an avoidance of decision making on basic planning needs of libraries."[113]

Librarians' century-long inability to determine and implement a viable role for the public library reflects an equally long-established lack of professional autonomy. The patrician men who filled the ranks of the first "generation" of public librarians were not without authority. Allied by their class background to library philanthropists and trustees and to other men of great wealth and power, they set goals for the library that were in keeping with their own class interests. It is with the late-century changes in the composition of the profession—upper class to middle class, male to female, "born" librarians to technically proficient "made" librarians—that librarianship came to accept externally imposed roles for its institution rather than generating a role of its own. This lack of autonomy with regard to the determination of a professional purpose represents a significant precondition of work alienation in that the profession has effectively lost control over the disposition of its "product" and is, in Marxist terms, thereby estranged from it. Habituated to surrendering control over the library's role to various representatives of sociopolitical authority and lacking professional unity and autonomy, we remain largely unprepared to determine the appropriate ends of our labor.

The lack of a clearly defined professional purpose contributes to role ambiguity at the levels of both the profession at large and the individual practitioner. Role ambiguity, by eroding the sense of meaning in one's work, further exacerbates the experience of work alienation and is a widely recognized precursor of burnout. It also reduces the professional confidence necessary for effective decision making, leading in turn to an even greater lack of autonomy.

A final effect of our failure to establish an autonomous professional purpose has been an ever-increasing professional absorption with technical details and an inability to distinguish between means and ends. Without an explicitly defined purpose, institutions are susceptible to a process known as goal displacement. A largely unconscious process, goal displacement is a gradual substitution of means for ends "through the day-to-day decisions which create more secure operational habits and minimize uncertainty, insecurity, frustration and risk."[114] Lacking a compelling mission, the profession has concentrated its attention on the technical details and bureaucratic imperatives of libraries to the extent that these have come to assume the stature of ends in themselves. Goal displacement "cuts an institution away from its philosophical moorings and sets it adrift."[115] The process alienates an institution and its personnel from the social milieu in which they exist because the institutional focus has been directed inward, emphasizing stability and stasis. Through its reification of means, displacement also reinforces lack of professional autonomy, thereby deepening the cycle as professional judgment and innovation become replaced by standardized procedures.

## NOTES

1. Dee Garrison, *Apostles of Culture: The Public Librarian and American Society, 1876–1920* (New York: The Free Press, 1979), p. xiii.
2. Michael H. Harris, "The Role of the Public Library in American Life: A Speculative Essay," Occasional Paper No. 117 (Champaign: University of Illinois, Graduate School of Library Science, January 1975), p. 6.
3. Clinton Rossiter, quoted in Michael H. Harris, *The Purpose of the American Public Library in Historical Perspective: A Revisionist Interpretation* (Washington, D.C.: ERIC Clearinghouse on Library and Information Sciences, 1972), p. 13.
4. Harris, *The Purpose of the American Public Library in Historical Perspective*, p. 14.
5. Ibid., p. 8.
6. Sidney Ditzion, *Arsenals of a Democratic Culture: A Social History of the American Public Library Movement in New England and the Middle States from 1850 to 1900* (Chicago: American Library Association, 1947), p. 108.
7. Harris, "The Role of the Public Library in American Life," p. 12.
8. Ditzion, *Arsenals of a Democratic Culture*, p. 108.
9. Rosemary Ruhig DuMont, *Reform and Reaction: The Big City Public Library in American Life* (Westport, Conn.: Greenwood Press, 1977), p. 20.
10. Garrison, *Apostles of Culture*, p. 44.
11. DuMont, *Reform and Reaction*, p. 52.
12. Garrison, *Apostles of Culture*, p. xii.
13. James Whitney, quoted in Garrison, *Apostles of Culture*, p. 39.
14. Garrison, *Apostles of Culture*, p. 39.
15. Ibid., pp. 16–17.
16. William Landram Williamson, *William Frederick Poole and the Modern Library Movement* (New York: Columbia University Press, 1963), p. 51.
17. Ibid., pp. 128–30.
18. Garrison, *Apostles of Culture*, p. 41.
19. Phyllis Dain, *The New York Public Library: A History of Its Founding and Early Years* (New York: New York Public Library, 1972), pp. 112–13.
20. Williamson, *William Frederick Poole and the Modern Library Movement*, p. 60.
21. DuMont, *Reform and Reaction*, p. 108.
22. Ibid., p. 109.
23. Harry Romaine, "The Censor," *Library Journal* 16 (June 1891): 168.
24. Sam Walter Foss, "The Library and Industrial Workers: Carry the Library to the Workers," *Public Libraries* 13 (March 1908): 82.
25. Sam Walter Foss, "Man More Than Machinery," *Public Libraries* 12 (April 1907): 120.
26. Harris, "The Purpose of the American Public Library in Historical Perspective," p. 28.

27. Garrison, *Apostles of Culture*, p. 162.
28. Ibid., p. 131.
29. Sarah K. Vann, ed., *Melvil Dewey: His Enduring Presence in Librarianship* (Littleton, Colo.: Libraries Unlimited, 1978), p. 77.
30. Ibid., p. 168.
31. Harris, "The Purpose of the American Public Library in Historical Perspective," p. 28; and Vann, *Melvil Dewey*, p. 90.
32. Williamson, *William Frederick Poole and the Modern Library Movement*, p. 102.
33. Carolyn M. Hewins, "Library Work for Women: Some Practical Suggestions on the Subject," *Library Journal* 16 (September 1891): 273.
34. Minnie Clarke Budlong, *A Plan of Organization for Small Libraries* (Boston: The Boston Book Company, 1917), p. 38.
35. Murray Levine, "Method or Madness: On the Alienation of the Professional," *Journal of Community Psychology* 10 (January 1982): 4.
36. Ibid., pp. 12–13.
37. Herbert E. Law, "The Public Library as a Business Proposition," *Library Journal* 30 (July 1905): 405.
38. Frederick Winslow Taylor, *The Principles of Scientific Management* (New York: Harper and Brothers, 1919), pp. 37–38.
39. Ibid., p. 19.
40. Ibid., p. 11.
41. Vann, *Melvil Dewey*, p. 91.
42. Garrison, *Apostles of Culture*, p. 169.
43. Ibid.
44. John Adams Lowe, *Public Library Administration* (Chicago: American Library Association, 1928), p. 2.
45. Floyd W. Reeves, "Some General Principles of Administrative Organization," in *Current Issues in Library Administration*, ed. Carleton B. Joeckel (Chicago: University of Chicago Press, 1939), p. 7.
46. Marshall E. Dimock, "The Place of Organization in Institutional Development," in *Current Issues in Library Administration*, ed. Joeckel, p. 78.
47. Douglas C. Basil and Curtis W. Cook, *The Management of Change* (Maidenhead, Berkshire, U.K.: McGraw-Hill, 1974), p. 61.
48. Richard M. Dougherty and Fred J. Heinritz, *Scientific Management of Library Operations* (New York: Scarecrow Press, 1966), pp. 75–76.
49. Richard M. Dougherty and Fred J. Heinritz, *Scientific Management of Library Operations*, 2nd ed. (Metuchen, N.J.: Scarecrow Press, 1982), p. 105.
50. Dougherty and Heinritz, *Scientific Management of Library Operations*, p. 17.
51. K. H. Jones, "Creative Library Management," in *A Reader in Library Management*, ed. Ross Shimmon (London: Clive Bingley, 1976), p. 56.
52. Herbert S. White, "Participative Management Is the Answer, but What Was the Question?" *Library Journal* 110 (August 1985): 63.
53. Jones, "Creative Library Management," pp. 51–52.
54. Williamson, *William Frederick Poole and the Modern Library Movement*, pp. 28–29.
55. Ibid., p. 28.
56. Garrison, *Apostles of Culture*, p. 173.

57. "The English Conference: Official Report of Proceedings," *Library Journal* 2 (January–February 1878): 280.

58. William I. Fletcher, *Public Libraries in America* (Boston: Roberts Brothers, 1894), p. 83.

59. Barbara Elizabeth Brand, "Sex-Typing in Education for Librarianship: 1870–1920," in *The Status of Women in Librarianship: Historical, Sociological, and Economic Issues*, ed. Kathleen M. Heim (New York: Neal-Schuman, 1983), p. 42.

60. Kathleen Weibel and Kathleen M. Heim, by *The Role of Women in Librarianship 1876–1976: The Entry, Advancement, and Struggle for Equalization in One Profession* (Phoenix: Oryx Press, 1979), p. 34.

61. Salome Cutler Fairchild, "Women in American Libraries," in *The Role of Women in Librarianship 1876–1976*, by Weibel and Heim, p. 54.

62. R. A. Storey, "Prospect and Prejudice, or Women and Librarianship 1880–1914: A Fourth Footnote," *Library History* 7 (No. 1, 1985): 22.

63. Melvil Dewey, "Women in Libraries: How They Are Handicapped," in *The Role of Women in Librarianship 1876–1976*, by Weibel and Heim, p. 10.

64. Fairchild, "Women in American Libraries," p. 54.

65. Garrison, *Apostles of Culture*, p. 178.

66. Ibid.

67. "Transactions and Proceedings of the Conference of Librarians Held in London, October, 1877," in *The Role of Women in Librarianship 1876–1976*, by Weibel and Heim, p. 5.

68. John MacFarlane, *Library Administration* (London: George Allen, 1898), p. 23.

69. Barbara Elizabeth Brand, "Librarianship and Other Female-Intensive Professions," *Journal of Library History* 18 (Fall 1983): 394.

70. Fairchild, "Women in American Libraries," pp. 51–52.

71. Suzanne Hildenbrand, "Ambiguous Authority and Aborted Ambition: Gender, Professionalism, and the Rise and Fall of the Welfare State," *Library Trends* 34 (Fall 1985): 191–92.

72. "Proceedings of the Fourteenth American Library Association Conference: The Woman's Meeting," in *The Role of Women in Librarianship 1876–1976*, by Weibel and Heim, p. 16.

73. Fairchild, "Women in American Libraries," pp. 53–55.

74. Dewey, "Women in Libraries," pp. 10–11.

75. Nancy Patricia O'Brien, "The Recruitment of Men into Librarianship, Following World War II," in *The Status of Women in Librarianship*, ed. Heim, p. 56.

76. Ibid., p. 65.

77. U.S. Department of Commerce, Bureau of the Census, *Statistical Abstract of the United States, 1987*, 107th ed. (Washington, D.C.: Government Printing Office, 1986), p. 385.

78. O'Brien, "The Recruitment of Men into Librarianship," p. 65.

79. Kathleen M. Heim and Carolyn Kacena, "Sex, Salaries, & Library Support . . . 1981," *Library Journal* 106 (September 15, 1981): 1695.

80. Garrison, *Apostles of Culture*, p. 192.

81. Ibid., p. 188.

82. Phyllis Dain, "Women's Studies in American Library History: Some Critical Reflections," *Journal of Library History* 18 (Fall 1983): 460–61.

83. Garrison, *Apostles of Culture*, p. 194.

84. Richard L. Simpson and Ida Harper Simpson, "Women and Bureaucracy in the Semi-Professions," in *The Semi-Professions and Their Organization: Teachers, Nurses, Social Workers*, ed. Amitai Etzioni (New York: Free Press, 1969), pp. 243–45.

85. Brand, "Sex-Typing in Education for Librarianship," p. 42.

86. Fletcher, *Public Libraries in America*, p. 80.

87. Garrison, *Apostles of Culture*, p. 190.

88. Charles C. Williamson, *Training for Library Service: A Report Prepared for the Carnegie Corporation of New York* (Boston: Merrymount Press, 1923), p. 25.

89. William Goode, "The Librarian: From Occupation to Profession?" *Library Quarterly* 31 (October 1961): 306–20.

90. Ibid., p. 316.

91. Mary Lee Bundy and Paul Wasserman, "Professionalism Reconsidered," *College and Research Libraries* 29 (January 1968): 5–26; Dale E. Shaffer, *The Maturity of Librarianship as a Profession* (Metuchen, N.J.: Scarecrow Press, 1968); Thomas Gwinup, "The Failure of Librarians to Attain Profession: the Causes, the Consequences, and the Prospect," *Wilson Library Bulletin* 48 (February 1974): 482–90; and John North, "Librarianship: A Profession?" *Canadian Library Journal* 34 (August 1977): 253–57.

92. "Statement on Professional Ethics, 1975," *American Libraries* 6 (April 1975): 231.

93. Thomas W. Shaughnessy, "Theory Building in Librarianship," *Journal of Library History* 11 (April 1976): 167–76.

94. Michael F. Winter, "The Professionalization of Librarianship," Occasional Paper No. 160 (Champaign: University of Illinois, Graduate School of Library and Information Science, July 1983), p. 32.

95. Bonnie R. Nelson, "The Chimera of Professionalism," *Library Journal* 105 (October 1, 1980): 2032.

96. William F. Birdsall, "Librarians and Professionalism: Status Measured by Outmoded Models," *Canadian Library Journal* 37 (June 1980): 146.

97. Ibid.

98. Beverly P. Lynch, "Libraries as Bureaucracies," *Library Trends* 27 (Winter 1979): 267.

99. R. C. Usherwood, "Professional Values in a Bureaucratic Structure," *Library Review* 29 (Spring 1980): 9.

100. Mary Lee Bundy, *Challenges to the System*, Urban Information Series Publication No. 2 (College Park, Md.: Urban Information Interpreters, 1972), p. 37.

101. Ibid., p. 41.

102. Lynch, "Libraries as Bureaucracies," p. 264.

103. Nancy Birch, Maurice P. Marchant, and Nathan M. Smith, "Perceived Role Conflict, Role Ambiguity, and Reference Librarian Burnout in Public Libraries," *Library and Information Science Research* 8 (January–March 1986): 62.

104. Simpson and Simpson, "Women and Bureaucracy in the Semi-Professions," p. 246.

105. Usherwood, "Professional Values in a Bureaucratic Structure," p. 9.

106. Michael H. Harris, "Portrait in Paradox: Commitment and Ambivalence in American Librarianship, 1876–1976," *Libri* 26 (December 1976): 284.

107. Ibid.

108. W. Caldwell, "Libraries and the Social Structure," *Assistant Librarian* 61 (October 1968): 217.

109. Public Library Association, Goals, Guidelines, and Standards Committee, *The Public Library Mission Statement and Its Imperatives for Service* (Chicago: American Library Association, 1979), p. 8.

110. Lawrence J. White, *The Public Library in the 1980s: The Problems of Choice* (Lexington, Mass.: Lexington Books, 1983).

111. Douglas L. Zweizig, "Lifelong Learning and the Library: The Public Library Response to *A Nation at Risk*," *Public Libraries* 23 (Fall 1984): 70–75.

112. Paul Wasserman, *The New Librarianship: A Challenge for Change* (New York: R. R. Bowker, 1972); Mary Lee Bundy, *Helping People Take Control: The Public Library's Mission in a Democracy* (College Park, Md.: Urban Information Interpreters, 1980); and Marcia J. Nauratil, *Public Libraries and Nontraditional Clienteles: The Politics of Special Services* (Westport, Conn.: Greenwood Press, 1985).

113. Spencer E. Watts and Alan R. Samuels, "What Business Are We In? Perceptions of the Roles and Purposes of the Public Library as Reflected in Professional Literature," *Public Libraries* 23 (Winter 1984): 133.

114. John R. Haak, "Goal Determination," in *A Reader in Library Management*, ed. Shimmon, p. 87.

115. Ibid., p. 88.

# 4

# Fuel for Burnout: Current Trends

For over a decade libraries have been increasingly challenged by fiscal crises, by demands for greater accountability from both funding sources and the public, by rampant technological development, and by competition from other suppliers of information. In response to these challenges, many libraries have acted in ways that alter the nature of the library both as a public service and as a workplace. The most far-reaching of these changes have resulted from the application of private sector ideologies and methods. This chapter addresses four major trends in librarianship and their consequences for public libraries, especially for those who work in them.

## THE FISCAL CRISIS AND AUSTERITY MANAGEMENT

Public libraries, whether integrated directly into the administrative structures of their municipalities (typically as city departments) or not, are dependent on their local governmental units for most of their income. This arrangement is often advantageous in terms of its cost-effectiveness and responsiveness to local concerns. Less favorable to the library is the precariousness of the local government's tax base.

Funding for public libraries has never been lavish. The institution's fortunes have risen and fallen in keeping with the economic times and the social attitudes engendered by them. Following a period of growth in the 1920s, libraries, like other local government agencies, found themselves in severely straitened circumstances during the thirties. Ann E. Prentice, an authority on public library finance, notes that bread, not books, was the priority of Depression-era municipal administrators.[1] The wartime economy of the early 1940s left little surplus for libraries, and it was not until publication of the Public Library Inquiry late in the decade that attention was focused on the need to plan for public library service. Libraries benefited from the general expansion of the economy in the fifties. The passage of the Library Services Act in 1956, authorizing direct federal support for public libraries, marked the beginning of a decade of unprecedented library development. Further federal funding was mandated in 1964 when the Library Services Act became the Library Services and Construction Act (LSCA). By the late 1960s, however, Washington was already beginning to be strapped for cash, and by the early seventies the gush of federal funds had become a sporadic trickle.

Municipal governments, caught in the squeeze of a contracting economy, faced a further crisis in the growing public cynicism toward all levels of government. Legislation such as California's Proposition 13 in 1978 and Massachusetts' Proposition 2½ in 1980 represents an increasing reluctance on the part of taxpayers to support public services. According to Princeton economist William J. Baumol, this trend is a logical consequence of the differential productivity potentials of the private and public sectors. While technology has allowed for massive productivity increases in manufacturing and agriculture, the labor-intensive nature of the service sector makes it less susceptible to such gains. As the economy moves from an industrial to a service orientation, lessened productivity increases are reflected in a slowed rise in the standard of living. The result is taxpayer indifference and even disfavor toward public sector spending, with no end to the trend in sight.[2]

In their attempts to reduce the demand on local revenue, municipal authorities have often applied a Depression-style system of triage, cutting back most severely on services they deem nonessential. When cities have been forced to reduce their budgets, libraries typically suffer more than other services. In New York City, for example, library service was cut 25 percent in the mid-1970s, while other municipal services were reduced by only 10 percent.[3]

At the same time that city hall has unleashed wolves to howl at their doors, public libraries have had to contend with greatly increased demands on their resources. While library expenditures increased only 4 percent in inflation-adjusted dollars between 1972 and 1982, circulation went up by 22 percent.[4] Salaries and benefits—which represent the major outlay in most library budgets—have increased substantially. A survey of eighteen medium- and large-size public libraries in the South indicates that average salaries of entry-level librarians, department heads, and library directors at least doubled between 1970 and 1983.[5] The cost of materials has escalated alarmingly during the same period. The average price of a hardcover book rose from $12.20 in 1973 to $31.22 in 1986. Magazine subscriptions increased from $16.20 to $65.00, a rise of 400 percent.[6] Computer-based library services are in ever greater public demand and have significant potential for both upgrading service and reducing some future expenditures. High start-up costs, however, have posed a dilemma to many libraries not unlike that faced by farmers during famine: whether to eat the grain intended to seed next year's harvest or save it and starve this winter.

Libraries have responded to the fiscal crisis in a variety of ways, with most adopting a combination of strategies. There has been a heightened awareness of the importance of political action, and many librarians have initiated or stepped up public relations activities, have sought the partisanship of influential groups, have become adept at grantsmanships, have mounted campaigns in favor of local bond issues, and have learned to lobby at the municipal, state, and even federal level. When traditional income sources have remained obdurately tight-fisted, some libraries have turned to more innovative forms of fund-raising. At least two libraries, Los Angeles Public and Mercer County Public in Harrodsburg, Kentucky, have added to their revenues through benefit basketball games.[7] In addition to their Buy-A-Book Campaign, Lincoln Library in Springfield, Illinois, has joined with Waldenbooks in a mutual profit venture. The library provides the bookstore with a desiderata list, benevolent library patrons purchase the items, and Waldenbooks types a bookplate for each donation and delivers it to the library. A similar relationship is being negotiated with a local computer store.[8] Other money-making schemes adopted by public libraries include the establishment of on-site book/gift shops, celebrity book and shoe auctions, a bellydancing competition, a Walk-A-Thon, and a fashion show.[9]

Despite determined efforts to halt the spiraling decline in library funding, many libraries have found themselves in deep financial waters. To keep themselves afloat, many have resorted to what is known variously as cutback management, contingency management, austerity management, retrenchment, or downsizing. The aim of austerity management is to reduce expenses and/or to increase productivity. It is based largely—and often unreservedly—on private sector management's belt-tightening percepts, which have come to be regarded with increasing favor by public sector managers. Many library administrators have already operationalized Prentice's recommendation that "new ways of defining the role of the public library and the way in which it uses it resources can be taken from the private sector."[10]

In a public sector version of corporate streamlining, many libraries have cut back on services. Branches have been closed, hours shortened, programs suspended, and moratoria imposed on purchase of materials. These cutbacks do not represent exercises in fat-trimming; unlike some government agencies, few public libraries ever found themselves in a position to indulge in extravagant waste. With personnel costs representing such a major share of the library budget, it is inevitable that they have appeared prominently on the chopping block. Some librarians have found themselves unexpectedly unemployed; many more have found their status suddenly altered to that of part-time employees, with their benefits sharply reduced or eliminated. Thomas Ballard, director of the Plainfield (New Jersey) Public Library, advises that "since the greatest expenditure is for staff, libraries should take advantage of all departures by leaving the vacancies open."[11] Economist Lawrence J. White advocates a more aggressive approach. Contending the library materials play a more important role in generating extra library use than is reflected by their position in the library budget, he argues that less money should be directed toward personnel and more toward materials.[12] Another economist, Malcolm Getz, is more businesslike still:

> If a library chooses to provide as much service value as possible within a given budget, it will substitute less expensive for more expensive activities. In particular, those libraries that face higher labor costs may be expected to adjust the mix of services so as to economize on the use of labor.[13]

The ruthless application of such purely economic criteria has transformed many corporations into "lean, mean machines" capable of turning a profit even in a contracting economy. Is it, however, an appropriate or even an efficient strategy for public libraries? Laurence E. Lynn, Jr., former federal government official and authority on public administration, maintains that the difference between public and private management is fundamental and irreconcilable:

> Whatever the similarities of task, activity, or even social setting, private management is oriented toward economic performance as determined in markets, whereas public management is oriented toward the public interest as determined in public forums. It is a difference in degree so great as to constitute a difference in kind.[14]

In business, the color of ink on the bottom line is the ultimate measure of success. Either profits are being made or they are not. In libraries, as in other nonprofit organizations, there is no such bottom-line measure. Success is more difficult to evaluate, involving qualitative as well as quantitative considerations. Does a 5 percent increase in circulation, for example, represent more value to the community and more effectiveness on the part of the library than a small but loyally attended program for seniors?

In addition to its potentially deleterious effects on quality of service, slashing the staffing budget has serious consequences for library personnel. There are fewer jobs and fewer opportunities for advancement. Morale is lowered, incentives are diminished, and job security—a traditional perk of public employment—is jeopardized. A formerly cooperative atmosphere of professionals working together can become charged with competitiveness as librarians maneuver to avoid the falling ax and push their way up narrowing career ladders. This heightened competition can result in a serious erosion of collegiality and is conducive to the same alienation that arises among industrial workers when the specter of unemployment forces them to relate to their fellow workers as threats to their own security. Career mobility, an important aspect of professional autonomy, also becomes circumscribed, and librarians' dependence on their present employer is deepened.

The imposition of fees for various services represents another attempt by the library to balance its budget and put itself on a more businesslike footing. User fees are not new. Libraries have long levied minor charges for photocopies, overdue materials, interlibrary loans, and book reservations. What is new is the concept of imposing fees as a means of expanding library service through expensive technology and of charging for basic service such as book loans in order to underwrite the library's regular operating costs. User-pay advocate Nancy A. Van House argues: "Without fees, the library is limited by its budget and limited to offering only those services for which the library can pick up the entire bill."[15] White recommends that the library adopt a "competitive-efficiency strategy," according to which fees would be charged to cover the marginal costs of each service as well as the library's overall costs.[16] Concern has been expressed that charging fees to increase library revenues may result in the library's shifting its attention from less lucrative services to those promising the best return.[17] This concern is borne out by White's positive view of the role fees might play in library decision making: "Libraries would have a guide for choosing among services, for allocating resources, for deciding when to buy duplicates, when to stay open longer hours, and what related services to provide."[18]

While profit-and-loss data may provide a logical and consistent blueprint for running a business, they are insufficient for managing a public organization. Lynn remarks that "a goal of numerous public programs is precisely to incur losses, to provide services that private firms could not provide at a profit."[19] While private executives are expected to concentrate solely on the profitability of their organizations, public administrators and the professionals who report to them must be concerned with the wider range of effects that their institution and its policies have on society. Thus, many librarians harbor misgivings about the effect on the poor of fees for library service and about the ways that this policy and other private sector policies may alter the public character of their institution. Management's expectations that it will enforce such policies as part of its professional duties compromise professional autonomy and can lead to significant levels of role conflict.

A further loss of professional autonomy results from the library's efforts to meet the other aim of the austerity agenda—increased productivity. In attempting to realize this aim, libraries have integrated many tenets and tactics from the private sector into their organizational routines. After years of often halfhearted commitment to the human relations approach to management and the more recent quality-of-worklife movement, there is a resurgence of interest in the seeming efficiency of scientific management. In their 1982 revised edition of *Scientific Management of Library Operations,* Dougherty and Heinritz cite the public demand for greater accountability and declare: "No, American taxpayers will not subscribe to the notion that scientific management applies only to profit-making firms!"[20] Increased workloads have become general. In many libraries, that hallmark of professional autonomy—regulating one's own time—has receded still further as employees' schedules reflect the need for remaining personnel to compensate for staff reductions. Time saving frequently takes precedence over professional expertise and inclination as librarians' duties are shuffled and reshuffled. At Denver Public, for example, specialist librarians have been demoted and stationed on the floor to serve the general public.[21] The new streamlined internal operations at California's Huntington Beach Library would move even Melvil Dewey and Frederick Taylor to admiration. After having divided various work processes "into component parts, analyzed how long each step should take, and, with the help of the employees involved, established criteria against which their performance would be measured, the system now runs like clockwork."[22]

Two other features of austerity management are notable for their potential effects on librarians and libraries. First, austerity management tends to be more autocratic and less open to staff input regarding institutional goals and methods. In his study of participative management in libraries, Donald Sager warns: "History will demonstrate that organizations in crisis usually centralize decision-making and policy determination. That is especially true in the public sector."[23] Reducing participation tends to increase work alienation. Second, austerity management, with all its attendant strains and disruptions, may not work after all. In his survey of proactive management in California libraries, Brian A. Reynolds suggests that cutback management has a built-in paradox: "Efficiency, effectiveness and increased production are required by local officials, by tax payers, and by the library profession. Yet, because there are no tangible pay-offs, retrenchment tends to work against such activities."[24] Librarians, deprived of the traditional job security of public employment, forced to relinquish substantial portions of their professional autonomy in furtherance of goals determined unilaterally by top management, and increasingly pressed to accelerate their productivity—in short, subject to all the tyrannies of the industrial speedup without the rewards that the private sector can afford to offer in compensation—may be expected to develop feelings of exploitation and cynicism regarding their work. The experience of work alienation under these circumstances is almost inevitable and may often be severe enough to manifest itself as burnout. Library effectiveness itself suffers in turn. The trimmed-down library is in danger of becoming dysfunctionally anorexic.

**AUTOMATION**

While library mechanization dates back to the sometimes inspired, often pettifogging practices of Melvil Dewey, library automation is generally considered to be synonymous with computerization. In his guide to library automation, Dennis Reynolds notes that reusability of data and flexibility in manipulating them constitute the technological foundations for automation.[25] The earliest machine to meet these criteria was invented in the late nineteenth century by American engineer Herman Hollerith. Combining a tabulator with a device for reading punched cards, the mechanical data processor soon became an office fixture. Later manufactured by IBM and other companies, such machines were incorporated into the circulation procedures of the University of Texas library as early as 1936, and they spread to many other libraries during the ensuing quarter-century. Use of machine-readable records remained sporadic, however, in acquisitions, serials control, and cataloging.[26]

The ballistics research of World War II produced the first decimal computer.[27] After that, development was rapid, spurred by the accelerating needs of the scientific and business communities. The transistor, the integrated circuit, and, eventually, the microchip increased the reliability and applicability of computers while lowering their costs. By the 1950s, computer use had spread from research- and development-related industries to insurance companies and banks.[28] In the following decade, pressured by increasing circulation and acquisitions activity, libraries began to install computers, primarily for off-line batch processing.[29] The development of minicomputers and the availability of bibliographic utilities such as OCLC (Ohio College Library Center) during the 1970s set the stage for on-line computer operations in libraries. The eighties witnessed the mushrooming of automated library systems, with 50 percent of the top academic and public libraries having automated catalogs, interloan, acquisitions, and circulation by mid-decade.[30]

Why have libraries embraced automation with such fervor? Some librarians have undoubtedly succumbed to the fear that avoidance of technology will result in our being "left to fade into oblivion in our museums full of books."[31] Most, however, have responded to more positive stimuli. Library automation is generally seen to have two major advantages—to improve service and to reduce or contain costs. There is little argument on the first point. Automation saves users time and increases their access to materials. Opinion regarding the financial aspects of automation is somewhat less sanguine. Michael Cart, city librarian, Beverly Hills Public Library, asserts that librarians consistently underestimate the costs of starting up and maintaining an automated system and that automation will not save money. "Once the piper starts playing, he must be paid. And paid. And paid."[32] Reynolds warns that even where an automated system reduces labor costs, it is also likely to introduce new time demands as tasks that were impossible or neglected under the manual system are initiated.[33]

In addition to the advantages that automation is considered to bring to the library and its users are its purported benefits to library staff. It has been claimed that automation increases not only worker efficiency and productivity but employment opportunities and job satisfaction as well. As Canadian librarian-sociologist Gale Moore points out, for those librarians involved in the early development of automated systems, the specialized skills that they acquired opened doors to new careers, whether in librarianship itself or within the information industry. Further, the introduction of computer searching enhanced librarians' prestige with library users, as librarians were perceived as possessing sophisticated technological skills. Both of these positive effects have been undermined by the subsequent diffusion of personal computers and computer literacy.[34] While some librarians report that automation has heightened their job satisfaction by reducing routine tasks, thereby making their work more interesting, others note that, once the novelty wears off, routine returns with a vengeance.[35]

Automation is changing the nature of the library as a workplace. While the changes are by no means all negative, the potential effects on library personnel are cause more for concern than for celebration. Expressions of this concern are increasingly heard at library association conferences and in the professional literature. At the 1983 Clinic on Library Applications of Data Processing, academic librarian Carolyn M. Gray remarked:

We are so enamored by the promises of the future applications and possibilities of technology that we lose sight of the human cataloger, serials clerk and the library patron. We promise increased a control and a decrease in the per unit costs of processing materials, but fail both to measure the human costs, and to assess the reality of the new application of technology.[36]

For many librarians, a fearsome reality of automation is its potential for job loss and staff displacement. In a Canadian study of 118 professional librarians and other library employees, 28 percent believed that automation leads to job loss and 31 percent that it results in job change.[37] Reynolds notes that when the costs of an automated system are lower than the costs of the manual system that it replaced, "savings are almost inevitably realized through staff layoffs or transfers to other departments in the library."[38] There is also a trend towards rehiring laid-off and new library workers on a part-time, contract, or temporary basis, not only to save on fringe benefits and unproductive time but to suit the computer's convenience.

Automation is a potent proletarianizer. In *Dreams Betrayed,* Carlton Rochell points out that much work is now organized to coordinate with the computer rather than to direct it: "As a result, workers are not only losing control over their work, they are also losing their understanding of it."[39] The deskilling that automation brings through intensified task specialization and fragmentation is considerable and is only partially mitigated by increased computer competencies. While it is sometimes argued that automation democratizes the workplace by blurring traditional authority hierarchies, this outcome more likely reflects a generalized loss of control rather than the deliberate diffusion of it. One librarian remarks that in her library, "automation has standardized decision making. This is an improvement over decisions made by various individuals within the department."[40] But while fiat by machine may seem more impartial than fiat by management, it leads to no gain in workers' decision-making power. Decisions that previously involved the exercise of professional judgment are not preprogrammed. In consequence, skills are degraded and professional autonomy compromised.

Automation is also proletarianizing because of the time constraints that it imposes. Machine pacing robs employees of all control over their own time and increases their vulnerability to speedups. The need to maximize use of computer time and the flexibility required for scheduling use of terminals have meant changes in working hours for many librarians. As one complains: "Access problems make it necessary to work at night; scheduling is a horrendous problem. As we depend more and more on the machine, we have to use it."[41] In order to take advantage of lowered costs and better response time during off-peak hours, library employees may be asked to "volunteer" for earlier or later shifts, or these may be assigned on the basis of seniority. Some libraries are staffed by computer-operator personnel twenty-four hours a day.[42] Many library managers have found their working day extended due to the "mobility of the office environment" that automation has created.[43] Particularly in a competitive employment market, it is increasingly difficult to leave work at the office when it is so easily accessible by personal computer at home, on business trips, even at the cottage.

The capital-intensive nature of automation makes it a tool of owners, employers, and administrators. As such, it has a great potential for reinforcing the power structure within organizations and for increasing the distance between those who manage and those who are managed. Psychologist Sara Fine notes that technology determines the high and low status that individuals hold in organizations, just as it separates the "have" from the "have-not" people in society. She further suggests that "technology is becoming one more male status symbol, once again unbalancing a hard-won professional and personal equality between the sexes."[44] Others have argued that the introduction of new office technologies stems as often from employers' desire to reinforce the patriarchal relations of control over office workers as from a concern for increased efficiency.[45] The computer's comprehensive tracking systems make it an effective instrument for employee monitoring and surveillance. Women clerical workers have reported anxiety arising from daily computer-generated records of their output and breakdowns of their time away from the machine.[46] Professional employees, too, are now more susceptible to computerized monitoring. While the ambiguous nature of much managerial and professional work had previously rendered it more or less immune to quantification, the recent development of management information systems and of various computer-related productivity measures has greatly extended the range of work subject to machine-trackable accountability.[47]

All of these ways in which automation modifies the nature of library work can deepen employees' experience of work alienation. Marx viewed increased alienation as an inevitable consequence of intensified production as alienation both extends the realm of alien powers to which individuals are subject and widens the gulf between workers and capitalists.[48] There is a growing recognition that automation can also induce alienation more directly, through the machine-human interaction itself.

Psychologist Craig Brod has coined the term "technostress" to denote "a modern disease of adaptation caused by an inability to cope with the new computer technologies in a healthy manner." Technostress manifests itself in two distinct but related ways, the more prevalent being anxiety over the pressure to use and accept computers.[49] People often express their technoanxiety by resisting or rejecting computer technology. They may sabotage the system by manually duplicating automated functions, thereby reducing its efficiency and increasing costs, or by more overt acts, such as entering incorrect data. Library managers may write disillusioned articles on automation.[50] An estimated 20 percent of library workers are actively or passively resistant to technology.[51] Fine argues that flexible, progressive individuals can be resistant as well as rigid traditionalists. While many technoanxieties are related to fears about job loss or ineptitude, Fine's research indicates that what people fear most is the potential breakdown of interpersonal relationships.[52]

At the other end of the spectrum from the technoanxious are the technocentered—individuals who overidentify with computers. While they may exude confidence and competence, Brod warns that "high performance with high technology can exercise a dangerous influence on the human personality by encouraging a symbiotic relationship with the machine," the primary symptom being "a loss in the capacity to feel and to relate to others."[53] The thoughts and behavior of technocentered people develop a mechanistic cast. They typically become obsessed with efficiency and speed and commensurately impatient with the vagaries of human behavior and communication. In a study of the effects of automation on special librarians, the programmers who were interviewed all reported personality changes related to increased use of computers in their work: "I'm impatient with unorganized, illogical people," and "I feel that my mind works like a computer now." Programmers reported difficulty in communicating with nonprogrammers and vice versa. One nonprogrammer librarian remarked: "We can explain what we want, but the programmers don't want to do it. They're used to dealing with scientific and mathematical data, not strings. And you can't talk to them like a normal person—you have to be totally precise and logical."[54] This schism between "technocrats and mandarins"[55] represents not only a case of workers' estrangement from each other but a serious threat to the professional cooperation necessary to an effective library service.

Automation can also have alienating effects on the librarian-client relationship. Brod relates the experience of Bill, a researcher, when he encountered the library's automated circulation system for the first time. Bill was often desultory in reaching the circulation desk before closing time but was generally able to persuade the librarian to bend the rules in his favor. When the new system was installed, the librarian explained that the matter was now out of her hands—the system would not accept a late transaction. " 'I started to yell at the librarian,' Bill recalls, 'which is unusual for me.' Because the computer had erased the normal bond between librarian and patron, Bill felt no compunctions about taking his anger out on the librarian."[56]

At bottom, system-induced alienation is less a matter of software and hardware than a matter of autonomy. Individuals' acceptance of automation is strongly influenced by their perception of the impact that it will have on their control over their work.[57] Job loss, staff displacement, deskilling, speedups, monitoring, even reduced employee interaction typically result from management's concern for increased efficiency, cost-cutting, or control rather than from any imperative derived from the equipment or its programs. While "high touch" activities can often buffer "high tech" stress to some extent, addressing computer-related work alienation means involving employees in the decisions whether, when, and how to automate. Even the hapless librarian upbraided by Bill would have been in more control of the situation had she had the discretionary authority to override her system.

## NONLIBRARIAN MANAGERS

The presence of experts from other fields is not a new phenomenon in the administrative offices of large public and academic libraries. Since World War II, the hiring of management consultants has been increasingly popular. Such consultants typically study various aspects of the library system that has employed them and then provide professional advice concerning salary and job classification, collection evaluation, physical planning, fund raising, or other administrative matters.[58] The role of management consultants is primarily advisory, their area of responsibility narrowly defined, their tenure relatively brief. While they may interview and consult with many members of the library staff, they typically hold no managerial authority.

In contrast to management consultants are permanent library administrators with backgrounds in business, personnel management, finance, or systems analysis rather than librarianship. These "imported managers" have been recruited increasingly in recent years by libraries and their governing bodies as the scale and complexity of library operations have expanded, especially in response to the fiscal crisis of the library and its growing reliance on automation. Municipal governments are demanding more and more evidence from libraries as to their efficiency and cost-effectiveness, while the rapid expansion of computer technology requires of library managers not only a modicum of technical expertise but an understanding of the legal, fiscal, and public policy issues related to resource sharing. Since few librarians have had the opportunity to develop these newly emphasized management skills through either their professional education or their "training in the ranks," the hiring of library managers from outside the profession has been seized upon as a quick solution.

There is little information available concerning the extent to which nonlibrarian managers are employed in public libraries. According to a survey reported in 1987, nearly two-thirds of the individuals holding "specialized administrative positions" (including personnel directors, public relations officers, and business managers) in large public libraries identify their profession as something other than librarianship. Most of the specialized administrators (93 percent) supervise other library workers as part of their duties, with just under half supervising professional librarians.[59] While this study excluded library directors, associate directors, and assistant directors from the sample, there are increasing references in the professional literature to the hiring of nonlibrarians for these positions as well.

Is the Midas touch of private sector managers the answer to the library's problems? As suggested earlier in the chapter, libraries, as public agencies, differ conceptually, organizationally, and economically from private businesses. Individual careerists in the private and public sectors also exhibit some fundamental differences. A study of graduate students in management found that the personalities, values, and behavior of individuals planning to join nonprofit organizations diverged significantly from those students anticipating corporate careers. Individuals oriented toward the public sector were more flexible, more interested in and skilled at being change agents, were better at personal relations, and demonstrated higher self-acceptance, social presence, and responsibility.[60] Professional education and work experience serve to widen the theoretical and practical gulf between public and corporate managers. The qualities and competencies that determine success in the private sector do not always transfer satisfactorily to the public sector. According to James Hodgson, a former businessman who became secretary of labor:

The most general of the reasons for the failure of successful businessmen in government is a lack of breadth—an inability to conceptualize rather than merely achieve, an inability to understand and be effective in the *relations* elements of a governmental role, and an inability to deal with problems indirectly rather than through authoritarian line control.[61]

Despite the constraints imposed by government commissions and public interest groups, corportate managers exercise a high degree of internal control over strategies, personnel, and resources. Spurred on by market competition and relatively unhindered by the political influences and public scrutiny that affect public agencies, private sector managers expect to wield great authority. The resulting management style is often frankly autocratic. As a former chairman of AT&T declared: "The purpose of the other managers in this company is to advise me. That's it. There can be only one person in an organization who makes policy decisions. In our case, that's me."[62] Even the most patriarchal of library administrators would shy away from making such a sweeping statement. Consider, however, the description of library teamwork by nonlibrarian Vincent Morehouse, who in 1980 assumed control of the Huntington Beach Library in California:

Walter [Johnson, the library's director] and his staff come up with ideas. . . . I review them, I'll have our analyst look at them, and we'll discuss them. If I feel they are good programs, I'll approve them, and if I don't—it's a checks and balances system—and if I don't approve them, they're dead.[63]

Accustomed to substantial personal authority and the gratification of immediate results, private sector managers are often frustrated by the relatively intangible goals and more diffuse power structure of nonprofit organizations. In their zeal to streamline internal operations, professional autonomy and participatory decision making are frequently jettisoned.

If the corporate manager's approach to decision making is often unpalatable to public sector professional employees, so are many of the decisions themselves and the criteria on which they are based. The bottom-line measure of success in the private sector is profit. When this model is superimposed on a traditionally nonprofit organization, that organization's own goals, structure, and character are jeopardized. One of Morehouse's decrees, for example (later rescinded in the face of public uproar), was to charge children admission to the library's story hour.[64] In this situation, significant conflict—including personnel role conflicts—is likely to occur.

When the public library imports managers from the private sector, it imports not only private sector expertise but private sector attitudes, methods, and goals. This orientation has long been implicated as a major cause of work alienation in industrial and white-collar employees and can be expected to exacerbate the experience of work alienation for public employees as well.

## MARKETING ORIENTATION

Libraries have long engaged in those activities known as advertising, promotion, publicity, and, more recently, public relations. In 1876, its inaugural year, *Library Journal* published an article by Samual Swet Green, librarian of the Worcester, Massachusetts, Free Public Library, extolling the advantages of establishing good librarian-community relations. These included stimulating readers' love of study, developing more relevant collections, popularizing the library, and strengthening its reputation.[65] While advertising was not without its detractors within the profession, libraries were soon enticing readers through acquisitions lists published in local newspapers or posted in prominent locations, mailed circulars, in-house displays and bulletin boards, and other strategies. Since the end of World War I, library literature has brimmed with tips and techniques for library publicity. National Library Week, established in the mid-1950s, has provided an ongoing focus for coordinated professional efforts to promote books and libraries.[66]

In the private sector, the luster of public relations has gradually dimmed in the rising of a new star—marketing. Its status has been reduced to that of a component part of the dominant marketing function. In *Marketing and Public Relations for Libraries,* Cossette Kies explains that "the value of both functions is recognized, but marketing is seen as the function which produces the desired bottom line result: profit; hence its importance."[67]

Nonprofit organizations, too, are turning to marketing as a potential solution to the problems posed by shrinking funds, underutilization, demands for accountability, and new competitors. An additional factor responsible for librarians' increasing involvement in market relations is the commoditization of information. The concept of knowledge and information as social goods to be used for the public benefit is rapidly being replaced with the concept that these are economic goods to be used for private gain.[68] In the words of a senior information technology scientist at AT&T Bell Laboratories, information "is no less a commodity than precious metals, pork bellies, or soybeans. . . . [It] can be advertised, promoted, marketed, and sold, just like other traditional tangible commodities."[69]

In his frequently cited text, *Marketing for Nonprofit Organizations,* Philip Kotler defines marketing as

the analysis, planning, implementation, and control of carefully formulated programs designed to bring about voluntary exchanges of values with target markets for the purpose of achieving organizational objectives. It relies heavily on designing the organization's offering in terms of the target markets' needs and desires, and on using effective pricing, communication, and distribution to inform, motivate, and service the markets.[70]

Kotler considers exchange to be the central concept underlying marketing. This principle is generally applied to libraries in terms of the materials and services that they offer in exchange for monies and support.[71] Andrea Dragon, who has written extensively on libraries and marketing, argues, however, that an exchange model is inadequate to describe what occurs in libraries and that it doesn't provide a sufficient incentive for placing marketing prominently in management planning. She modifies Kotler's definition by proposing that marketing should be viewed as a competition for prizes:

It is based on the idea that both nonprofit organizations and businesses exist solely to win prizes and that these institutions exist to get such things as museum memberships, concert subscriptions, blood donations, or increased funding from fiscal authorities. . . . Every competition has winners and losers and . . . only the market will decide which one of these lies in store for the library.[72]

Libraries have traditionally been product-oriented. The materials, programs, and information that comprise the library's product have been assumed to be of value to the library's constituency, and promotional efforts have been directed toward increasing public awareness of this value. In contrast, the market-oriented organization identifies the needs and desires of various market segments, develops products and services to appeal to selected segments, and then promotes them. Adopting a marketing orientation implies a fundamental change in the concept and practice of public librarianship. It represents the superimposition on a public service agency of not only private sector methods but private sector ideologies. In a classic reversal of ends and means, marketing is being touted as the appropriate dominant function of libraries as well as businesses. In the words of a management consultant: "As heretical as it may seem in these times, marketing probably deserves financial preference over the more basic library activities."[73] And from within the profession itself: "In these days of tight budgets and a stress upon accountability, the library that chooses marketing must often turn away from such traditional practices of librarianship as building balanced collections or attempting to preserve the best of the world's knowledge."[74]

Within a marketing context, library users are transformed from clients and constituencies with needs deserving of satisfaction for their own sake to market segments with needs perceived as exploitable for the benefit of the organization. These organizational benefits, whether viewed as "prizes" or as direct exchange, generally take the form of enhanced resources and support leading to ensured self-perpetuation. This conversion of information needs from worthwhile ends in themselves into mere means to organizational ends presents a serious challenge to our professional values and an alienating influence on the librarian-client relationship. Exacerbating the effect is the emphasis that marketing places upon market segmentation. As it has developed in the private sector, marketing involves creating products to satisfy one or more distinct market segments. If a particular segment is considered to be unresponsive or unprofitable, it is ignored.[75] This concept has carried over into public sector marketing. Kotler states unequivocally: "Marketing means the selection of target markets rather than a quixotic attempt to serve every market and be all things to all men."[76] Echoing Kotler, Dragon maintains: "As simple practicality, libraries need not and should not attempt to appeal to every segment of the market."[77] Such blithe disregard for certain sectors of the library's constituency—most likely those that have been traditionally underserved—is blatantly at odds with the "service to all" philosophy to which most librarians profess allegiance. This incongruity may come to represent a significant source of role conflict as more and more librarians find their libraries becoming market-oriented.

The emphasis that marketing places on managerial control poses a threat to librarians' control over their work. Kotler defines marketing as a managerial process.[78] Kies insists that "control of the entire process must be centered at the management level."[79] Some believe that library marketing is better taken out of the hands of librarians entirely and left to the expertise of marketing professionals.[80] Since its proponents also tend to regard marketing as the library's proper dominant function, adoption of a marketing orientation can be expected both to narrow the scope of professional practice and to reduce workplace democracy.

Another alienating aspect of the marketing orientation lies in its essential compatibility to the privatization and commoditization of information. The majority of United States data-base producers and vendors are private firms.[81] The title of the 1986 Information Industry Association Annual Meeting—"Making Money with Information"—leaves little doubt as to why these firms are in business.[82] In the big business that information has become, the products don't come cheap. As a Louisville attorney complains: "When a search is not billable to the client, we use books. . . . Online's just too expensive."[83] While on-line information services began as speedy alternatives to print sources, an increasing quantity of information now bypasses print entirely to appear directly in electronic form, allowing the information-rich to purchase not only quicker access to data but privy information as well. Observes the executive from AT&T Bell Laboratories: "It is now clear that marketplace forces, rather than individual needs, drive the development and introduction of new information products."[84] For market-oriented libraries, it is a great temptation to select those market segments that will result in the greatest "return" for the library. These segments will almost certainly be those that are willing to pay for on-line services. For many librarians, this selection means a further loss of control over work objectives and procedures as their professional judgment is ultimately usurped by the law of supply and demand.

## NOTES

1. Ann E. Prentice, "Public Libraries," in *The Bowker Annual of Library & Book Trade Information,* 29th ed., comp. and ed. Julia Ehresmann (New York: R. R. Bowker, 1984), p. 63.
2. Thomas Ballard, "Public Library Finance: An Economic Forecast," *Wilson Library Bulletin* 57 (February 1983):471–74.
3. Prentice, "Public Libraries," p. 64.
4. "Fat Circ Figures No Fluke, Goldhor Survey Figures Show," *Library Journal* 108 (September 15, 1983):1750.
5. Prentice, "Public Libraries," p. 64.
6. Hugh C. Atkinson, "Prices of U.S. and Foreign Published Materials," in *The Bowker Annual of Library & Book Trade Information,* 19th ed., ed. Madeline Miele (New York: R. R. Bowker, 1974), pp. 208, 210; and Rebecca T. Lenzini, "Prices of U.S. and Foreign Published Materials," in *The Bowker Annual of Library & Book Trade Information,* 32nd ed., comp. and ed. Filomena Simora (New York: R. R. Bowker, 1987), pp. 435–36.
7. "LAPL's $10 Million Drive Hits the Halfway Mark," *Library Journal* 112 (February 1, 1987):23; and "Hoops for Books Nets Big Points for Library," *American Libraries* 14 (January 1983):8.
8. James Larue, "No Dough: How to Manage When Money Is Tight," *Illinois Libraries* 69 (February 1987):111.
9. "Library Funding," *Library Journal* 108 (January 15, 1983):96; and "LAPL's $10 Million Drive Hits the Halfway Mark," p. 23.
10. Prentice, "Public Libraries," p. 66.
11. Ballard, "Public Library Finance," p. 474.
12. Lawrence J. White, *The Public Library in the 1980s: The Problems of Choice* (Lexington, Mass.: Lexington Books, 1983), p. 89.
13. Malcolm Getz, *Public Libraries: An Economic View* (Baltimore: Johns Hopkins University Press, 1980), p. 37.
14. Laurence E. Lynn, Jr., *Managing the Public's Business: The Job of the Government Executive* (New York: Basic Books, 1981), pp. 114–15.
15. Nancy A. Van House, *Public Library User Fees: The Use and Finance of Public Libraries* (Westport, Conn.: Greenwood Press, 1983), p. 120.
16. White, *The Public Library in the 1980s,* pp. 144–145.
17. Fay M. Blake, "What's a Nice Librarian Like You Doing Behind a Cash Register?" in *User Fees: A Practical Perspective,* ed. Miriam A. Drake (Littleton, Colo.: Libraries Unlimited, 1981), p. 46.
18. White, *The Public Library in the 1980s,* p. 146.
19. Lynn, *Managing the Public's Business,* p. 126.
20. Richard M. Dougherty and Fred J. Heinritz, *Scientific Management of Library Operations,* 2nd ed. (Metuchen, N.J.: Scarecrow Press, 1982), p. 8.
21. "Denver Public Makes Changes to Halt a Long Decline," *Library Journal* 111 (May 15, 1986):17.
22. Donald Newman, "Vincent Morehouse—He Means Business," *Wilson Library Bulletin* 57 (February 1983):489.
23. Donald J. Sager, *Participatory Management in Libraries* (Metuchen, N.J.: Scarecrow Press, 1982), p. 176.

24. Brian A. Reynolds, "Proactive Management in Public Libraries—in California and in the Nation," in *Advances in Library Administration and Organization: A Research Annual,* vol. 6, ed. Gerard B. McCabe and Bernard Kreissman (Greenwich, Conn.: JAI Press, 1986), p. 16.

25. Dennis Reynolds, *Library Automation: Issues and Applications* (New York: R. R. Bowker, 1985), p. 5.

26. Ibid., pp. 15–17.

27. Carlton Rochell, *Dreams Betrayed: Working in the Technological Age* (Lexington, Mass.: Lexington Books, 1987), p. 11.

28. Ibid., p. 16.

29. Reynolds, *Library Automation,* p. 22.

30. Karl Nyren, "*LJ* News Report, 1986," in *The Bowker Annual of Library & Book Trade Infomation,* 32nd ed., comp. and ed. Filomena Simora (New York: R. R. Bowker, 1987), p. 11.

31. Carolyn M. Gray, "Technology and the Academic Staff or the Resurgence of the Luddites," in *Professional Competencies: Technology and the Librarian,* ed. Linda C. Smith (Urbana-Champaign: Graduate School of Library and Information Science, University of Illinois, 1983), p. 69.

32. Michael Cart, "Caveats, Qualms, and Quibbles: A Revisionist View of Library Automation," *Library Journal* 112 (February 1, 1987):41.

33. Reynolds, *Library Automation,* p. 209.

34. Gale Moore, "Reassessing the Social Impacts of New Technology," *Canadian Library Journal* 44 (December 1987):423–24.

35. Ganga Dakshinamurti, "Automation's Effect on Library Personnel," *Canadian Library Journal* 42 (December 1985):348.

36. Gray, "Technology and the Academic Staff," pp. 69–70.

37. Dakshinamurti, "Automation's Effect on Library Personnel," p. 349.

38. Reynolds, *Library Automation,* p. 209.

39. Rochell, *Dreams Betrayed,* p. 18.

40. Dakshinamurti, "Automation's Effect on Library Personnel," p. 348.

41. Julie Bichteler, "Human Aspects of High Tech in Special Libraries," *Special Libraries* 77 (Summer 1986):125.

42. Margaret Myers, "Personnel Considerations in Library Automation," in *Human Aspects of Library Automation: Helping Staff and Patrons Cope,* ed. Debora Shaw (Urbana-Champaign: Graduate School of Library and Information Science, University of Illinois, 1986), p. 40.

43. Bichteler, "Human Aspects of High Tech in Special Libraries," p. 122.

44. Sara Fine, "Terminal Paralysis, or Showdown at the Interface," in *Human Aspects of Library Automation,* ed. Shaw, pp. 5–13.

45. Amy Wharton and Val Burris, "Office Automation and Its Impact on Women Workers," *Humboldt Journal of Social Relations* 10 (Spring-Summer 1983): 112–26.

46. Heather Menzies, *Women and the Chip: Case Studies of the Effects of Informatics on Employment in Canada* (Montreal: The Institute for Research on Public Policy, 1981), p. 63.

47. Rochell, *Dreams Betrayed,* p. 48.

48. James W. Rinehart, *The Tyranny of Work: Alienation and the Labour Process,* 2nd ed. (Toronto: Harcourt, Brace Jovanovich Canada, 1987), p. 14.

49. Craig Brod and Wes St. John, *Technostress: The Human Cost of the Computer Revolution* (Reading, Mass.: Addison-Wesley, 1984), p. 16.

50. Larry W. Osborne, "Satisfaction with Library Systems," in *Advances in Library Administration and Organization: A Research Annual,* vol. 4, ed. Gerard B. McCabe and Bernard Kreissman (Greenwich, Conn.: JAI Press, 1985), p. 57.

51. Fine, "Terminal Paralysis," p. 4.

52. Ibid., p. 5.

53. Brod and St. John, *Technostress,* p. 17.

54. Bichteler, "Human Aspects of High Tech in Special Libraries," pp. 125–26.

55. Joseph Rosenblum, "Technocrats and Mandarins: The Two Cultures of Librarianship," *The Southeastern Librarian* 31 (Summer 1981):68–70.

56. Brod and St. John, *Technostress,* p. 19.

57. William B. Rouse and Nancy M. Morris, "Understanding and Enhancing User Acceptance of Computer Technology," *IEEE Transactions on Systems, Man, & Cybernetics* 16 (November-December 1986):965–73.

58. Richard M. Dougherty, "The Role of Management Consultants in the 1980s," *Library Trends* 28 (Winter 1980):425.

59. Barbara M. Morgan and Peter A. Neenan, "The Public Library's Invisible Managers," *Library Journal* 112 (June 15, 1987): 27–29.

60. James R. Rawls, Robert A. Ullrich, and Oscar Tivis Nelson, Jr., "A Comparison of Managers Entering or Reentering the Profit and Nonprofit Sectors," *Academy of Management Journal* 18 (September 1975):616–23.

61. James Hodgson, quoted in Lynn, *Managing the Public's Business,* p. 122.

62. John deButts, quoted in Lynn, *Managing the Public's Business,* p. 134.

63. Newman, "Vincent Morehouse—He Means Business," p. 489.

64. Ibid., p. 487.

65. Cosette Kies, *Marketing and Public Relations for Libraries* (Metuchen, N.J.: Scarecrow Press, 1987), p. 18.

66. Ibid., p. 28.

67. Ibid., p. 10.

68. Moore, "Reassessing the Social Impacts of New Technology," p. 421.

69. Donald T. Hawkins, "The Commodity Nature of Information," *Online* 11 (January 1987):67–68.

70. Philip Kotler, *Marketing for Nonprofit Organizations,* 2nd ed. (Englewood Cliffs, N.J.: Prentice-Hall, 1982), p. 6.

71. Anne J. Mathews, "The Use of Marketing Principles in Library Planning," in *Marketing for Libraries and Information Agencies,* ed. Darlene E. Weingand (Norwood, N.J.: Ablex Publishing, 1984), p. 4.

72. Andrea C. Dragon, "The Marketing of Public Library Services," *Drexel Library Quarterly* 19 (Spring 1983):122–23.

73. Daniel Carroll, "Library Marketing: Old and New Truths," *Wilson Library Bulletin* 57 (November 1982):216.

74. Kies, *Marketing and Public Relations for Libraries,* p. 48.

75. Michael L. Rothschild, "Marketing Communications in Nonbusiness Situations or Why It's So Hard to Sell Brotherhood Like Soap," in *Marketing for Libraries and Information Agencies,* ed. Weingand, p. 43.

76. Kotler, *Marketing for Nonprofit Organizations,* p. 7.

77. Dragon, "The Marketing of Public Library Services," p. 130.

78. Kotler, *Marketing for Nonprofit Organizations,* p. 6.
79. Kies, *Marketing and Public Relations for Libraries,* p. 84.
80. Carroll, "Library Marketing," p. 214.
81. Moore, "Reassessing the Social Impacts of New Technology," p. 421.
82. Hawkins, "The Commodity Nature of Information," p. 68.
83. Stephen E. Arnold, "End-Users: Dreams or Dollars," *Online* 11 (January 1987):78.
84. Hawkins, "The Commodity Nature of Information," p. 68.

# 5

# Coping and Beyond

> Noli in spiritu combueri.
> (Refuse to be burnt-out.)
>
> The Fugs

Work can exalt the human spirit or reduce it to a pile of burnt-out rubble. Work that involves the autonomous use of individuals' innovative and creative abilities results in personal and professional growth and in the satisfaction that comes from making a meaningful contribution to one's society. Work designs that ignore or deny workers' human needs and potentials set the stage for work alienation and burnout. Unfortunately, as Studs Terkel remarks, "most of us have jobs that are too small for our spirit."[1]

## EFFORTS TOWARD WORK REFORM

Working conditions in nineteenth-century factories and offices were generally abysmal and not infrequently resulted in serious industrial accidents and fires. Public outcry and pressure by the popular press led to the passage of Workmen's Compensation Acts by a number of state legislatures beginning in 1911. These laws, by fixing the responsibility for accidents squarely on employers, forced a widespread improvement in working conditions.[2] Another early impetus toward work reform was the organized labor movement. In addition to its struggles for equitable compensation, union bargaining has been responsible for the establishment of many health and safety regulations, for the adoption of the forty-hour workweek, and for such worker benefits as vacations, sick leave, and pensions.

Increasing union militancy, worker discontent, and the labor shortages of World War I, coupled in some cases with genuine employer humanitarianism, gave rise to the welfare management movement. Predicated on the belief that comfortable working conditions lead to greater productivity, welfare management provided employees with amenities ranging from washrooms to company housing, athletic fields, and libraries. Concurrent with Taylorism and contradictory to many of its tenets, welfare management was never widely adopted, and a rise in unemployment in 1921 provided a final disincentive to employers to continue costly welfare programs.[3]

The celebrated Hawthorne studies, carried out at the Western Electric Company between 1924 and 1939, marked the beginning of the human relations movement in personnel management. These experiments, originally designed to measure the impact of altered illumination, suggested that virtually any indication of managerial interest in worker well-being resulted in both increased productivity and job satisfaction—a serendipitous discovery that the researchers dubbed the "Hawthorne Effect." This brought to light the importance of employee attitudes. Physical environment issues were soon eclipsed as research, theory, and management methods came to focus on the psychology of the worker.[4] Proponents of human relations viewed urban workers as anomic and lacking a sense of community. It was the responsibility of "socially skilled" managers, they believed, to make workers feel they "belonged." Expected bonus effects were boosted productivity and greater harmony between workers and management. These principles of human relations management in many cases degenerated into such paternalistic cant as "the firm is just one big happy family," provoking criticism from both the left and the right and a growing reluctance for industrial investigators to associate themselves with the movement.[5]

The "neo-human relations" school that arose in the 1960s represented yet another shift in the focus of work reform. While workers' psychosocial needs remained a key concern, the appropriate locus of intervention was now considered to be the organizational setting itself. Rather than trying to modify workers' attitudes toward their work, proponents urged changes in work design.[6] In this step, they foreshadowed the current quality-of-worklife movement (QWL).

QWL, also known as work humanization or the new industrial relations, has different meanings for employers, union leaders, researchers, and workers. According to industrial psychologist David Bowers, "Perhaps the best that can be said for the moment is that [it] refers to work activities that are congruent with human needs and desires, and our concern with this problem reflects a feeling that in this day and age the alignment is not very good."[7]

The term "quality of worklife" was first publicly adopted at an international symposium on work problems in 1972.[8] QWL encompasses any number of workplace innovations, but the movement has had two major thrusts.

The first of these is job redesign. The most common form of job redesign is "enrichment" or "enlargement," in which repetitive, fractionalized jobs are broadened to include more task variety and often responsibility for larger units of production. While the factory assembly line has been the most obvious target of job redesign programs, efforts have been directed at white-collar work as well. In an early and extensive redesign project, AT&T "enriched" the jobs of over 4,000 employees between 1965 and 1968. One restructured job was that of complaints clerk. Formerly, clerks were required to respond to customers' complaints by using a standard format. These form letters were signed by supervisors after being checked by verifiers. In their revised jobs, the clerks were allowed more latitude in responding to customers, signed their own names to letters, and had only a small sample of their work checked.[9]

The second major thrust of the quality-of-worklife movement has been toward participative management. Worker participation can range from slipping ideas into a suggestion box to codetermination—shared decision making between labor and management. Quality circles represent an increasingly popular approach. Originally the brainchild of American industrial consultants in the 1950s, these small committees of management and labor representatives allow joint analysis and solution of various production problems and work-related issues. While quality circles were widely adopted in Japan, the concept languished in North America until the mid-seventies.[10] Another approach is the autonomous work team, a self-directed group of workers who plan their own activity, assign work internally, and promote and discipline their own members.[11] Between one-third and one-half of America's Fortune-500 companies have reportedly adopted some form of participative project.[12]

Worker participation and the broader QWL movement are widely considered vital by both labor and management, if from somewhat different perspectives. United Auto Workers spokesman Irving Bluestone views QWL as synonymous with basic human rights:

Unless we can democratize the workplace as we have democratized other aspects of our society, our future looks dark. More importantly, we will be missing that level of potential which is possible for humans to reach. It is my belief that in the years ahead . . . as workers are increasingly given responsibility to make their own decisions within the framework of what needs to be produced, this will strengthen our society, not weaken it. It will mean that the worker in our democratic society has come into his own *in the shop* as he has in the other aspects of his life.[13]

To H. Ross Perot, architect of a sweeping reorganization program at General Motors in the mid-1980s, employer humanitarianism is measurable in terms of profit and loss:

In many of our huge corporations we treat people like commodities. And people cannot be managed. Inventories can be managed, but people must be led. And when people are reacting to being treated improperly, they are not doing their best work. And when they're not doing their best work, our international competitors can beat us.[14]

This discrepancy between the expectations of labor and those of management has meant obstructions and delay to the QWL movement. North American unions, unlike their more politicized European counterparts, have been reluctant to embrace codetermination goals, fearing that this step might compromise their traditionally adversarial stance. From a management perspective, resources are rarely committed to QWL programs without the hope of a tangible return. While most companies welcome increased cooperation from their employees, few are willing to grant workers true autonomy in their work or to diffuse policy-making authority. As economist Sar A. Levitan remarks: "The desire of managers to elicit worker participation and thus achieve greater productivity while preserving traditional decisionmaking preogatives creates the fundamental tension in quality-of-worklife schemes."[15]

More serious criticisms have been leveled at management involved in QWL programs than simply that they want to have their cake and eat it too. Industrial sociologist Michael Rose cites research suggesting that 80 percent of QWL schemes in the United States contain as a hidden agenda the inoculation of workers against unionism.[16] Canadian sociologist James Rinehart charges that "work humanization" is often merely a euphemism for "work rationalization." In the case of the AT&T clerks, for example, the increased variety of their "enriched" jobs also involved a substantial increase in their workloads—in essence, speedup. The consolidation of clerical tasks, verification, and minor supervisory duties rendered the jobs of many first- and second-line supervisors redundant, saving the company thousands of dollars annually in salaries. In another case, plant management found that production of fiberglass yarns was running at only 65 percent efficiency because of the need to stop the machines periodically for cleaning by special crews. The solution was job enlargement. Machine operators were taught to clean their own machines, a change that eliminated both the cleaners' salaries and machine downtime. Rinehart contends that many redesign programs do not significantly alter job content or workplace authority relations. "Even if we grant that forms of job redesign reduce repetitiveness and alleviate boredom, task variability is not the *sine qua non* of challenging non-alienated work. The critical determinant of an intrinsically gratifying job is the control over work exercised by individuals and groups of workers."[17] Even when participation is a stated QWL objective, employers typically grant workers discretion only in how they pursue company ends not in how they can help to shape management policy.[18]

Is work reform a dead letter? For economic and cultural reasons, its progress has been rockier and its success more limited in North America than in Europe and Japan. QWL *has* had the effect of raising the expectations of employees regarding their working conditions and general treatment by their employers. Further, the principles contained within QWL provide a blueprint, as yet largely unacted upon, for reducing workplace alienation and designing jobs that are consistent with democratic and humanistic goals.

## CONFRONTING WORK ALIENATION AND BURNOUT

The consequences of work alienation—and its end state, burnout—can be devastating for individuals, for organizations, and for society. Recognition of the seriousness of the problem has generated a great deal of advice and some research as to how it might be ameliorated. Much, if not most, of this attention has focused at the individual level, in keeping with the widely held view that burnout is primarily an individual problem. Thus, psychologist-counselors Nancy and Donald Tubesing assert that "the most potent force in the burnout equation is the suffering individual whose own internal wisdom can be activated to diagnose and alleviate the symptoms."[19] With only a cursory nod in the direction of structural factors, psychologist Beverly Potter also advocates that individual practitioners try to heal themselves: "While the large solution requires a broad-based alteration in the organizational structure and environment, this is an unrealistic hope at this time. Clinging to such an expectation is folly: you may burn out first!"[20]

The pervasiveness of this individual approach to burnout has spawned a large and lucrative stress-management industry. Theodore Barash, founder of Stresscare, a Long Island-based consulting firm, predicts bullishly that "in the next 10 years, stress can be a $15 billion industry."[21] While techniques differ, the various programs and workshops target their intervention at the individual, coaching him or her in how to adapt to or cope with the stresses of workplace and occupation. The popularity of these stress-management and burnout programs among employers can be ascribed to the promise of a "quick fix." Arrangements are easily made with private consultants, and at that point the responsibility of management is at an end. No changes of the work environment are required.[22]

But are individual efforts effective at curing or reducing the severity of burnout? A growing body of research indicates they are not. In a 1978 study, which has become a model for subsequent research, 2300 people were interviewed to determine the efficacy of individual coping in various problem areas. It was found that while individual coping often succeeds with marital and parenting problems and with problems involving household economics, it has little effect on occupation-induced strains. The authors concluded that many human problems, including those related to work, are deeply rooted in social and economic organization and, as such, may be responsive only to collective interventions. Given the structural nature of these problems, individual coping "at best provides but a thin cushion to absorb the impact of imperfect social organization."[23] Burnout researchers Ayala Pines and Elliot Aronson found most of the individual coping strategies used by a sample of human service and management professionals to be unsuccessful in preventing burnout.[24] A longitudinal study of 517 Chicago area adults reported in 1984 had similar results: "While some coping efforts altered the negative feelings associated with one's work conditions, these individual coping efforts had no direct or indirect impact on problem change."[25]

Particularly convincing are the findings of another 1984 study, based on data collected from 141 human service workers (psychologists, social workers, pastoral counselors, and nurses). A wide range of individual coping strategies was reported, including focusing attention on family and friends or hobbies rather than the job, attending conferences, talking to coworkers, and introducing greater variety into the work routine. Respondents also reported on strategies that their agencies had adopted for reducing job stress and burnout. The individual coping efforts were found to have no ameliorative effect on any of the strain measures, which included job dissatisfaction, alienation, and somatic and psychological symptoms. On the other hand, strategies applied at the group and agency levels *were* effective in reducing both job dissatisfaction and alienation. Interestingly, while respondents suggested many strategies that agencies could adopt, very few agencies had actually taken any steps in this direction. The investigators concluded that "little is to be gained by exhorting human service professionals to change their ways, because individual coping has little impact on job strain."[26]

As social work educator Rebecca Donovan points out, given the general ineffectiveness of individual coping on occupational stress and burnout, the emphasis on stress management places an unrealistic and unfair burden on individual workers.[27] It also deflects attention from organizational and social-structural solutions, delaying needed change. At the same time, the very prominence of individual coping strategies warrants their consideration. Individual coping can be a useful component of a multilevel approach or may be the only option available for some librarians experiencing burnout. Finally, some individual coping strategies are better than others.

## Individual and Collegial Coping

Coping has been defined as "the things that people do to avoid being harmed by life-strains."[28] In most of the occupational stress research, individual coping strategies are classified as primary, secondary, or tertiary. Primary responses, aimed at modifying or eliminating the source of stress, represent the most direct form of coping. Confronting one's supervisor or in some way changing one's job falls into this category. Secondary responses do not address the problem itself but the worker's perception of it. Secondary coping strategies include "counting one's blessings" or trying to ignore unpleasant realities. Tertiary coping involves the management of the physical and emotional symptoms that have already emerged as the result of job stress—for example, relaxation techniques, massage, and meditation. Numerous research studies demonstrate that only primary coping strategies have any effect on occupational stress and burnout.[29] Nevertheless, the individual coping strategies most often resorted to are secondary and tertiary ones.[30]

The most recommended, most used, and least effective individual approach to work-related stress is tertiary coping—symptom management. Prescribed under this rubric are rest, breaks, relaxation, hobbies, and television viewing. Hot water is considered a sovereign specific; burnt-out individuals are routinely advised to indulge in hot baths, hot tubs, saunas, and jacuzzis. Physical exercise, "perhaps the most popular form of individual stress reduction in our society today," is touted not only as a means of relieving tension but as a means of "strengthen[ing] our body and organs so that we are better able to withstand the onslaught of future stress."[31] Yoga, massage, and diet modification all have their advocates. Biofeedback and visualization techniques are popular at workshops. Burnout authority Christina Maslach recommends "decompression activities," which allow workers to unwind and leave the job behind before becoming fully involved with family and friends. These activities again might include hobbies, sports, reading, saunas, naps, and massage.[32] Should all of these methods prove insufficient, the burnt-out individual is exhorted to try self-hypnosis, meditation, hope, and prayer to reduce the negative effects of stress.

As with symptom management, the purpose of secondary coping is to cushion the experience of work alienation and not to modify or eliminate its source. Human service workers are encouraged, above all, to develop "realistic expectations." Burnout researchers Jerry Edelwich and Archie Brodsky equate this attitude with "living with the 'givens' ": "The more one's expectations are in line with reality, the less frustration one will suffer. . . . Expect to be doing a difficult job without sufficient resources or outward rewards."[33] Workers are encouraged to "accentuate the positive," to focus on their successes, to concentrate on process rather then on results.[34] Other secondary strategies are based on the premise that by reducing the significance of work in one's life, one also reduces the impact of work alienation. Individuals are advised to set new priorities, emphasizing the importance of family, friends, and leisure pursuits. Emotional overinvolvement with one's work is roundly condemned. Two burnout authorities even recommend a rigid compartmentalization between work and the other spheres of life. "This compartmentalization enables people to be involved in each one of the roles they play and yet to limit the stresses inherent in those roles to their time and place."[35] Modifications in the approach to one's work are suggested not as a step toward job redesign but as a means of improving one's attitude. Thus Maslach remarks: "By choosing to do things in different ways and varying your work routine, you can get out of that rut and feel more in control of your job."[36] Pines and Aronson go so far as to urge workers to aspire to "flow experiences." Citing as an example the chess master who is so absorbed in the game as to be oblivious to external stimuli, these researchers contend that "while very few people play chess or paint as an occupation, it is also the case that there are very few occupations that are so barren as to not include some possibility for the creative individual to find a way to flow, at least some of the time, on the job."[37]

It is clear why secondary and tertiary coping strategies are ineffective in dealing with burnout. Increasing television viewing and compartmentalizing the different arenas of one's life are hardly sound antidotes to alienation. Accepting the alienating, or even the merely irritating, aspects of the job as non-negotiable "givens" can only reinforce workers' feelings of helplessness, reducing still further their opportunities for autonomy. Expecting a person who sits in front of a video display terminal for eight hours a day or who has just explained the intricacies of the *Readers' Guide* for the fifteenth time in a morning to attain a mystical peak is insulting as well as unrealistic. There is some evidence that secondary and tertiary coping strategies are not only ineffective but actually harmful. In a study of managers and medical professionals reported in 1986, both secondary and tertiary strategies were associated with an increase in psychosomatic symptoms.[38] Maslach recounts the experience of several groups of nurses who learned and practiced relaxation techniques. A follow-up indicated that those nurses making most use of the techniques were also having the most work-related problems. What went wrong? Apparently, the nurses overestimated the positive effects of the relaxation techniques, felt that they could now "handle anything," and accepted increasing amounts of work and responsibility. According to Maslach, "instead of alleviating stress, this coping strategy exacerbated it."[39]

Primary coping is the one self-help strategy that has been shown to be of some use in reducing work alienation and burnout. There are limits, certainly, to the impact that an individual can have upon institutional procedures. Even so, burnout experts seem unduly reluctant to encourage workers to "take the bull by the horns." Maslach, for example, cautions against pitting one's energy against things that are "institutionally fixed" until one has successfully tackled the "less formidable" aspects of one's job.[40]

The following tactics that might be employed by an individual worker are presented in ascending order in terms of directness and control and also in terms of personal risk. A relatively common individual strategy is to attend conferences and continuing education programs as a means of increasing competence and building confidence. Less common is confronting one's supervisor regarding alienating aspects of one's work—overload, lack of autonomy, and inconsistency between organizational and professional expectations. A librarian might object, for example, verbally or in writing, to the imposition of a three-minute limit on reference contacts. A stronger tactic is actually to resist procedures that compromise professional autonomy, such as speedups and personnel shufflings that result in deskilling. A librarian might refuse overtime or unusual shifts occasioned by automation. He or she might decide not to terminate reference contacts until the required information is transferred, even if the three-minute limit is violated. An even more direct assault on the source of work alienation is to agitate within the library for job redesign and participative management.

Perhaps the most dramatic individual strategy is to change jobs. The most typical change for human service workers is to move into administration (the major career ladder for librarians) or to establish a career in professional education. Some entrepreneurial spirits opt to leave the organizational context of librarianship to become independent consultants or information brokers. A more extreme decision is to leave the profession entirely. Despite the enormous time pressures and financial uncertainty of operating a small business, to many burnt-out professionals the lure of being their own boss is irresistible. Others may train to enter a new profession. As Edelwich and Brodsky point out, until quite recently, women were channeled into traditionally female professions—teaching, nursing, social work, and librarianship—with little regard for their aptitude or disposition. The new opportunities in the private sector, often made available through affirmative action programs, have encouraged many women to leave unsatisfying human service jobs for business careers.[41] Such a career change does not represent a surefire cure for burnout, of course; work alienation permeates the private sector at least as profoundly as it does the public sector. Still, the increase in career options affords women workers more chance for self-determination and may mean that those now entering the human services do so as the result of a freer exercise of choice.

Collegial or group coping—often referred to as social support in the occupational stress literature—represents an essentially quantitative advance over individual coping. Social support generally results not in modifying or eliminating the source of work alienation and job stress but in buffering their effects. While the research is far from unanimous, most studies do show that social support is negatively associated with burnout.[42]

While support may come from one's family and friends, work-related stress is most successfully mitigated by support from coworkers and supervisors. Support can be either socioemotional or instrumental. Esteem, affection, sympathy, and understanding are components of socioemotional support.[43] Colleagues can provide each other with recognition and praise, with a shoulder to cry on, and with escape from routine. A particularly important form of socioemotional support is the sharing of social reality—the external validation of one's perceptions.[44] This collegial coping mechanism generally leads to the relieved realization that "I'm not the only one who feels like this."

Instrumental support encompasses more concrete forms of collegial assistance. These include sharing information, insights, and advice, helping with work-related burdens, and covering for one another. Many of the primary individual strategies can also be adopted by groups of coworkers; with the show of greater strength, the confrontation, position paper, or refusal to abide by organizational policy will have a greater chance of success.

While both socioemotional and instrumental collegial support can be exchanged on an informal basis, they are often structured within the context of staff support groups. The group may be formed from an already existing unit—a work team, for example, or a library's technical services department—or its members may be drawn from throughout the organization. Staff support groups can be initiated by the agency or by workers themselves. They are generally scheduled at regular intervals and are run along lines of a discussion group, although they can sometimes more closely resemble therapy groups. While catharsis and examination of feelings are important support group functions, the most effective staff support groups are those adopting a problem-solving approach.[45] Maslach warns against the danger of group meetings' degenerating into "bitch" sessions.[46] Psychologist Cary Cherniss is also ambivalent. Asserting that burnout can be highly contagious, he cautions that when professionals who are already burnt-out get together to discuss their feelings and experiences, the outcome could well be more burnout. Even when collegial support does result in reduced stress for staff members, it can be detrimental to the professional-client relationship. This effect occurs when support groups engage in ridicule of clients—librarians, for example, have been known to joke about the "imbecility" of users who appear to lack familiarity with the alphabet—promoting a dehumanizing emotional detachment from them. Whether staff support groups ultimately help or harm depends on how they are structured: "If the feelings of members are accepted and they are helped to go *beyond* the expression of feeling, to formulate constructive attitudes and behaviors for dealing with problems, the support group can be a powerful method for alleviating burnout."[47]

### Organizational Change

A consistent finding of occupational stress research has been that intervention at the organizational level can be highly effective in reducing work alienation and burnout. Despite this finding, some burnout authorities—the majority of whom are psychologists, whose professional paradigm emphasizes individual pathology—are less than wholehearted in their endorsement of organizational change as a solution to the burnout dilemma. One team of researchers contends that "although organizations can promote a climate that minimizes the pressures leading toward burnout, they cannot totally prevent it or cure it once it has occurred."[48] Pines agrees that a work environment without burnout is probably an impossible goal, given the individual strengths, weaknesses, and coping strategies that workers bring to the job. And yet, "while individual differences may determine how soon one will burn out, how extreme the experience will be, and what will be its consequences, the work environment determines the likelihood of burnout across the board."[49] For Cherniss, the workplace represents "an obvious and necessary point for intervention."[50] Even given such advocacy, the burnout literature is full of recommendations for band-aid solutions, stopgap measures, and workplace modifications that are merely cosmetic in nature. Few discussions focus on worker autonomy and control, the hallmarks of professional work and the basic requisites of nonalienated labor. The following discussion addresses a variety of organizational strategies, concluding with a consideration of how professional autonomy can be maximized within the context of participative management.

Some proposed organization-level strategies simply call for agency sanctioning or facilitating of individual coping. An example is the orientation program, designed to cushion fledgling professionals from disillusion resulting from their unrealistic expectations. According to Cherniss, "work places that hire the new professional can alleviate reality shock and burnout through carefully planned orientation programs based on what has been learned about the most typical strains experienced by new public professionals."[51] In fact, however, recent research suggests that unrealistic expectations may not play the significant role in burnout that has long been assumed.[52] Another recommended organizational intervention is the "burnout checkup." This would be conducted by an individual with no administrative authority over the staff members being evaluated, and the results would have no bearing on pay raises or promotions. The purpose of the burnout checkup is to "assess the current levels of stress, strain, commitment, and satisfaction with work and identify factors that might lead to a decline in commitment and motivation in the future." If the person were found to be "at risk," an individualized course of "corrective action" would follow.[53] Burnout workshops, discussed earlier, are widely considered worthwhile organizational interventions. Individual counseling is also recommended. Maslach proposes that current definitions of job-related problems be expanded to include burnout, so that therapy can be covered under employee health insurance plans. She also recommends that support services be made available to the staff member's family.[54] While all of these interventions are to be applied at the institutional level, none represent any modifications to either organizational structures or the work that is carried out within them. These measures may help certain individuals to cope with their symptoms, but they are unlikely to have any wider impact beyond, perhaps, the "Hawthorne Effect."

For libraries and other public agencies, a more potent organizational strategy against employee burnout may be obtaining more resources. In these times of widespread undervaluing of social services, this strategy is admittedly a daunting proposition. Community action, seeking the support of influential groups, writing grant applications, and lobbying state legislatures are time-consuming and uncertain conduits to increased funding. But the potential benefits to library employees, and indirectly to library users, are compelling. Increased revenues mean more staff, more facilities, more time, and more materials. With such a belt-loosening, the assembly-line mentality of austerity management could be allowed to recede, along with its speedups, overloads, deskilling, surveillance, and other workplace tyrannies.

Better funding would also make it easier for libraries to increase the level of employees' extrinsic rewards, including salaries, benefits, and job security. Rewards can enhance workers' sense of the significance of their work, while lack of adequate rewards has been found to be an important correlate of burnout among professional workers.[55] Job security, a traditional perk of public sector employment and a perk now seriously eroded, has also been found to have a strong positive influence on employees' physical and mental well-being.[56]

Increasing the level of employees' intrinsic rewards, including support, recognition, and appreciation, can also be a useful strategy. Although imposing little burden on the library's financial resources, it does require ongoing organizational commitment. Poor relations with supervisors are strongly associated with job dissatisfaction and burnout, while high levels of feedback tend to mitigate their effects.[57] Supportive feedback not only reassures workers about their achievements and provides them with encouragement, but the increased communication reduces social isolation, can help clarify problems of role conflict and ambiguity, and can enhance workers' sense of meaning.

The bulk of the organizational strategies recommended in the literature on burnout can loosely be classified as job redesign or job enrichment. Improving the physical quality of the work environment to facilitate both the work itself and social interaction is a basic measure. Applications range from the superficial (painting the staff lounge a cheery orange) to the architectural (providing librarians with personally designed offices). Crowding, architectural dysfunction, and noise are the most common work environment stressors.[58] Since individual needs, preferences, and tolerance levels vary, the optimum approach would involve sufficient organizational flexibility to allow workers to modify their own workspaces.

Focusing more directly on the job itself, most burnout authorities emphasize the importance of variety and of increased flexibility in work routines. Collegial sharing of tasks, job rotation, lateral job transfers, and cross-training are all means to this end. A more specific recommendation, based on the conviction that "people work" represents a key stressor leading to burnout, is to structure jobs so that the public contact component of the work is shared equally among staff members. Maslach contends that if everyone is assigned both public contact and administrative chores, work that is emotionally draining will be counterbalanced by work that is not.[59] These organizational strategies can be considered only partially effective. While variety can reduce tedium, it cannot of itself reduce work alienation. As in the corporate sector, there is also a danger that libraries, particularly under austerity management, may transgress the line between variety and overload. Responsibility for administering a new program of films and book discussions at local senior citizen centers, for example, may be less enriching than exhausting for an already overworked librarian. Further, the negative emphasis on public contact may be misplaced. In a study of human service workers, interaction with difficult clients did not emerge as a prominent predictor of strain, while inadequate supervision and lack of agency support and recognition did.[60] Other research suggests that the most burnt-out workers may actually be those who spend a large share of their time on paperwork and administrative duties.[61]

These same criticisms can be applied to a related strategy, also premised on the assumption that work involving public contact is uniquely stressful. This strategy calls for organizations to increase staff members' opportunities for time-out. These can range from extra coffee breaks to conference attendance, vacations, and sabbaticals. An increasingly popular innovation is the "mental health day," distinct from sick leave and taken at the worker's discretion. Implicit within this strategy of officially permitted "escapes" is the recognition that the job, for whatever reason, is detrimental to workers' well-being. As with individual symptom management coping, however, effects can be at best merely palliative, as the underlying problem remains unresolved.

Having a greater potential effectiveness against burnout are proposals for ways in which organizations can modify work to make it less alienating. Pines and Aronson address this issue from the perspective of "completion." They liken social workers who do only intake interviews and never see positive changes in their clients to auto workers who weld on only front fenders and never participate in producing a whole car. "A sense of completion is unfortunately lacking in many industrial assembly-line jobs, as well as in human service jobs involving chronically sick or needy people."[62] Librarians can only rarely experience the satisfaction that comes from knowing that the information that they have provided has meant positive changes in users' lives. This lack exists because we do not monitor library users as hospitals do patients or as social service agencies do welfare recipients. The issue of completion is a salient one, however, in light of the increasing fragmentation and deskilling of library work. Pines and Aronson suggest that clear, achievable organizational goals and periodic evaluation can contribute to workers' sense of completion.[63]

Another strategy to enhance workers' sense of completion and, more broadly, of meaning in their work is the reduction of bureaucratic interference. Excessive rules and regulations, arbitrary policies, red tape, and paperwork have all been found to correlate positively with burnout.[64] Bureaucratic hierarchies also create communication problems that increase workers' isolation and alienation. Library directors may be six or seven links up the chain of command from some workers and unfamiliar with the problems that these workers are experiencing. Flattening the hierarchical structure can reduce this problem.

All of the foregoing organizational strategies represent ways in which management can intervene in employees' worklives to make them more tolerable. Pleasant working conditions, reduced paperwork, time-out, variety, and clear organizational goals can buffer job stress and help individuals to feel better about their work, as can the more obvious compensations of adequate pay, job security, and official recognition. None of these strategies, however, have much of an impact on the facts of worklife. Employees, even professional employees, are essentially told what to do and how to do it. They ordinarily have little autonomy over their own increasingly narrow spheres of operation, much less a voice in organizational policy.

In the research on burnout and occupational stress, lack of autonomy has consistently emerged as a major, if not the leading, causal variable. It is generally acknowledged by burnout authorities to be a key stressor. Yet increasing workers' control over their work is rarely proposed as a solution to burnout. When autonomy is recommended as an organizational strategy, it is in terms of a slight managerial slackening of the reins; workers should be "granted" a "degree" of autonomy. Maslach, one of the first and possibly the foremost burnout authority, discusses autonomy in very narrow terms:

Many of the strategies for coping with burnout are, in fact, strategies for personal power. . . . The person changes the work routine, redefines goals, utilizes downshifts, takes breaks, seeks out positive feedback, engages in decompression activities, and so forth. All of these actions involve *choice* and *initiative*—the hallmarks of freedom and autonomy.[65]

This is timid stuff indeed. The essence of autonomy is not to be able to decide which way to squirm in one's straitjacket but to be able to take it off.

Professional autonomy implies direct control over one's own work and direct or representative influence upon organizational policies. In order to increase professional autonomy in any way that is not merely superficial, changes in the authority structure of the organization are required. These changes involve the decentralization of decision-making power. The resulting configuration is known variously as participative management, collective management, self-management, and workplace democracy.

Political scientist Ronald Mason defines workplace democracy as "that type of workplace rule in which the process of decision making generally entails widespread and effective participation of workplace members."[66] In order to meet the first condition, participation must extend to all individuals employed by the organization. In libraries, this extension means the inclusion of clerical workers, pages, managers, and consultants as well as professional librarians. Mason's second condition refers to the impact that workers' participation has on organizational decisions. If management can ignore staff recommendations, then there is no genuine participation in decision making.

Studies on workplace democracy in settings as diverse as the Israeli kibbutz industry, the nationwide system of worker-managed enterprises of Yugoslavia, and American corporations and social service agencies indicate that it significantly reduces work alienation and enhances the intrinsic value of work.[67] Research focusing on librarians has arrived at similar conclusions. In his 1970 investigation of twenty-two academic libraries, Maurice P. Marchant found management style and, particularly, the degree of librarian participation in management decisions to be of special significance in both librarians' job satisfaction and productivity.[68] Marchant concluded that increased participation yields higher staff job satisfaction, which in turn exerts a positive effect upon productivity. "The results of the research are very clear. . . . Service is better in libraries that involve the staff in their management than in libraries run by authoritarian methods."[69] A 1985 study conducted at the Brigham Young University Library found that as librarians' participation in management increases, so does their satisfaction with the university administration, with their supervisors, and with their opportunities for professional growth.[70] Conversely, low individual influence on library policies and procedures has been linked to burnout among corporate librarians.[71]

Despite the empirical evidence that democratizing the library can be of substantial benefit to employees and users alike, implementation has proceeded at a much slower pace than in the private sector. Few public libraries in North America have embraced participative management. More academic libraries have introduced some degree of democratization into their management structure, as these libraries have been influenced, no doubt, by the collegial model characteristic of university faculties. Even where participative management is employed, it has often assumed the form of an administrative style rather than that of a genuine workplace democracy. Sometimes library directors adopt consultative management—inviting input from staff members while continuing to make all or most decisions themselves—believing this to be true participative management.

Some of this foot-dragging is attributable to the same factors that have hampered workplace democracy in the private sector. Many library executives, like their corporate counterparts, have been reluctant to share authority with their subordinates. There is also some concern that participative management could make the role of library director redundant, although as yet no participatively managed library has passed out pink slips to its administrative staff.[72] While the superiority of collective over individual decisions has constituted a basic tenet of participative democracy since the days of Aristotle,[73] it is still argued that managers are trained decision makers, who should thus enjoy a monopoly in their unique skill. Library educator Herb White worries that weak managers will abdicate their responsibility to committees to avoid making risky decisions.[74] Some resistance to democratization has emanated from librarians themselves. As Donald Sager points out in his monograph, *Participatory Management in Libraries,* librarians have not, historically, been militant employees. While this fact is changing, many librarians continue to believe that as professionals they should not involve themselves in labor-management issues, including workplace democratization.[75] Finally—and in these days of retrenchment, perhaps more telling—there is the economic argument. While participative management has been shown to boost both performance and job satisfaction, the economic benefits are hard to measure, and the costs are all too clear. One possibly unanticipated expense results from the necessary increase in intra-organizational communication. If employees are to make decisions, they must have access to pertinent information. This access requires the reproduction and distribution of budget documents, policy drafts, and personnel reports. A house journal in which staff can share information is also useful but not inexpensive; the preparation, printing, and distribution of a monthly newsletter to its two thousand employees costs the Chicago Public Library an estimated $24,000 annually.[76] The more obvious cost is staff time. Projected mimimum requirements range from one hour every week or two per involved employee to "a halftime position and extensive training."[77]

The most common vehicle of participation in libraries is the committee. Some are standing committees; many others are struck on an ad hoc basis to plan for one-time events, such as redecorating the staff lounge, introducing automation, or sponsoring a black writers' festival. According to Sager, "the best advice on comittee structure is to keep the number of standing committees to a minimum, and rely more on ad-hoc groups."[78] He argues that this arrangement will increase participation—a weak claim given that the membership of most standing committees is subject to rotation. His other rationales, that this arrangement will "keep the number of groups in control" and "reduce problems of monitoring the independent actions of committees," are more ominous. Structuring workplace democracy to suit the bureaucratic convenience of management is self-defeating.

Quality Circles (QCs) can be an effective adjunct or, in some cases, alternative to library committees. QCs are similar in structure to standing committees, generally being composed of five to ten members plus a leader selected by circle participants. They differ in that they are ordinarily organized at the level of the production unit (in libraries, this is most often the department) and that membership is completely voluntary and nonrestrictive. The typically permanent status of the QC and the cohesion among its members—who generally work closely together, or whose work is at least closely related to that of other group members—foster confidence and facility in problem solving.

The Duluth (Minnesota) Public Library established QCs in 1981. They include both professional and clerical staff and have dealt with issues ranging from building security, CRT (cathode ray terminal) hazards, and software updates for the circulation and on-line cataloging systems to improvement of user-staff relationships.[79] Taking a different approach, the East Brunswick (New Jersey) Public Library established a QC to generate solutions to a specific problem—overcrowding during peak periods. Once the problem was resolved, the quality circle disbanded—much like a conventional ad hoc committee—though a future circle will be involved in the library's planning process for building expansion.[80]

While in the private sector QCs frequently include both workers and management personnel who jointly have the authority to make decisions on production-level matters, library applications and literature have emphasized all-worker QCs that ultimately present recommendations to management for approval. This form of quality circle can still lead to effective participation, but only if management has a strong commitment to implementing QC recommendations whenever possible. The production-level organization and focus of quality circles limit their utility as a means for participation in policy-level decision making. A more serious problem with QCs is that they may encourage workers to adopt a managerial perspective (possibly to the detriment of their own self-interest) and may weaken workers' attachment to their union.[81]

Autonomous (and semi-autonomous) work teams provide a vehicle for higher levels of worker control and participation in decision making. Originally designed as an alternative to the assembly line, wherein a small group of industrial workers plan and assemble an entire automobile or other product, semi-autonomous teams have also been tried successfully in a social service setting. As part of a demonstration project funded by the National Institute of Mental Health, services to seniors were restructured in a family agency. Two control groups were organized in the traditional, centralized, hierarchical structure. Social workers in the control groups were assigned caseloads and had no direct control over ancillary workers who provided services to their clients. Two semi-autonomous teams were organized in a decentralized manner; caseloads were assigned to the team rather than to individuals, and the teams included homemakers and other ancillary staff. As might be expected, team workers felt they were more in control of their caseloads and experienced more peer support and autonomy. They also reported less isolation and alienation than control group staff. Team members were found to provide higher levels of supportive counseling to clients, while the conventionally organized workers tended to distance themselves from clients by shortening contracts and interviewing by telephone. Most surprising, the semi-autonomous teams reduced operating costs, as their flexible structure allowed for more efficient deployment of different staff levels. The researchers concluded that "one of the strongest effects of the team is to reduce burnout on caseloads where there are many difficult cases."[82]

The autonomous work team represents a qualitative advance over other organizational approaches to work alienation and burnout. Sociologists Charles Derber and William Schwartz argue that "unlike individual job enrichment programs, semiautonomous teams directly increase workers' experience of the social character of production and provide them with unique opportunities for developing capacities for cooperative shop-floor decision making."[83] The conceptual basis of autonomous work teams is that by dividing the work enterprise into small, relatively independent functional units—virtually into separate workplaces—high levels of participation are facilitated.[84] In the library, these functional units would probably be at the departmental level, though in large libraries subdepartmental work teams would be less unwieldy and allow for more direct participation. In the adoption of this form of participative management, as many decisions as possible are devolved to the autonomous work group, whose members ideally exercise complete control over all intra-unit matters. These would include the planning of activity, division of labor, quality control, enforcement of rules, and even the hiring and firing of unit members.[85] Absolute autonomy is impracticable, of course, as the teams must coordinate with each other, and each must contribute to organizational goals. Thus, the circulation department work group cannot unilaterally decide to eliminate evening shifts, as this decision would adversely affect other work groups and organizational effectiveness. The need for intergroup coordination can be met through a committee of unit representatives or by administrative personnel acting as facilitators and liaisons.

Workplace democracy requires, in addition to maximum worker autonomy, direct or representative influence by individuals on organizational policies. Nominal degrees of influence can be accomplished through such devices as the suggestion box, while higher quality influence is achievable through committees and quality circles—if management is responsive. The surest route, however, is codetermination, "a system whereby worker representatives are granted voting privileges at the board level."[86] In the corporate sector, true codetermination implies a board composed of equal numbers of labor and stockholder representatives. In a public agency like the library, there are other constituencies to consider, most notably the users. Changing the composition of the public library board is long overdue, if only because their members are rarely representative of the library's community. A general restructuring can be the opportunity for adding representation from both community groups and library staff. This change may, in some cases, require amending current library legislation. In Europe there is a solid tradition of legislation regarding codetermination. The West German system of *mitbestimmung* ("having a voice") established parity between worker and stockholder representatives in the coal, iron, and steel industries following World War II. In 1976 this parity was extended by law to all companies with more than 2,000 employees. The same year, Sweden required all companies employing more than twenty-five people to include two worker directors on their boards. In Austria, firms with more than 300 workers must have boards composed on one-third worker representatives.[87] Danish regulations, enacted in 1967, guarantee public library staff certain participative management prerogatives as well as the right to make proposals and statements directly to the political authorities.[88]

These three forms of participative management—quality circles, autonomous work teams, and codetermination—are complementary and reinforcing. With some modification they should be feasible in any type of library, though participation is more easily achieved in small and medium-sized libraries than in very large ones. Where the library is unionized, the collective bargaining unit should be involved in all phases of planning and implementation.

One caveat must be stated. Effective as participative management is in reducing work alienation and its end state, burnout, its impact is ultimately limited by the capitalist social system in which it must operate. Corporate managers and owners are typically tolerant of workplace democracy insofar as it increases employee integration and productivity but quickly turn implacable when they perceive their own prerogatives becoming vulnerable to "mob rule." As Poul Andersen and Børge Sørensen point out in their account of collective management in Danish public libraries, workplace democracy is a more viable objective in publicly owned institutions because the stumbling block of private ownership is missing.[89] Nevertheless, the public sector in North America has traditionally been both influenced by capitalist economic principles and subject to the dictates of a capitalist-dominated state, a tendency that is redoubled in times of economic uncertainty or crisis.

### Involving the Profession at Large

Profession-level efforts toward the prevention and elimination of librarian alienation and burnout have a high potential effectiveness. It is here that agendas are set, policies and guiding philosophies are endorsed, and opinions and attitudes are shaped. Three major forces can be mobilized at this level: library associations, library unions, and library education.

State, regional, and national library associations can foster recognition and understanding of professional alienation by featuring the topic at conferences and in their publications. Professional debate can be stimulated through the formation of committees and round tables. Since other professions—notably teaching, nursing, and social work—have a head start on librarians in their campaigns against burnout, collaboration and coalition will be of great value; library associations represent an obvious vehicle for such cooperative efforts. By encouraging and sponsoring research and demonstration projects, library associations can play a leadership role in generating solutions to the problem of alienated labor in libraries. Library associations can also adopt and promote recommendations and guidelines emphasizing the importance of professional autonomy and ways it can be maximized. Finally, library associations can lend their support to the development of library unions.

Professional workers—especially semi-professionals, whose work and status are most vulnerable to the eroding effects of proletarianization—are joining labor unions in increasing numbers. This trend toward union membership stems from the growing recognition that individual workers, whether pipe fitters or math teachers, wield little power or influence. Only through collective action can they improve their chances for economic and social justice in the workplace.

The first public library union was organized at the New York Public Library in 1917.[90] Unionization in libraries spread for the next three years as it did throughout the economy, then declined in the twenties, and rose again during the Depression. A third wave of library union development began with the social and labor unrest of the 1960s and continues to expand.[91]

Labor organization in libraries has assumed a variety of forms. Some librarians have established small in-house unions, generally known as staff associations. These rarely provide true union representation.[92] Others have affiliated with national labor unions such as AFSCME (American Federation of State, County, and Municipal Employees) and labor confederations such as the AFL-CIO. Librarians have also joined local and regional unions that cut across occupational categories within specific governmental levels (for example, municipal employee unions).[93] This fragmentation of library unions is often attributed to the profession's small size, which forces affiliation with other occupational groups. Another factor is the heterogeneity of labor relations legislation. While private institutions (including many university libraries) come under federal jurisdiction, public libraries are subject to state and local statutes.[94]

Library unions have been effective in raising the salaries of library workers.[95] Collective bargaining in libraries is also associated with better fringe benefits and fairer grievance procedures.[96] Nevertheless, only a minority of the profession are union members. The fragmented state of library labor organization is partly responsible, but ideological resistance has also proven to be a major stumbling block. From the days of the first library unions, debate has raged over their appropriateness. The sacrosanctity of the profession has been continually evoked; librarians have expressed concern that union involvement will reduce the status of librarianship, jeopardize the attainment of professional goals, and compromise the professional's service orientation. Experience with unionization, however, tends to allay such anxieties, rejected with eloquence by Washington State librarian William P. Tucker as long ago as 1939:

> Public servants are coming to realize that they are not untrue to the public weal, when they align themselves with the rest of the labor movement to improve their own conditions and promote the welfare of their occupation. The American labor movement is the true representative of the hopes, aspirations, and interests of the great majority of our population. . . . Professionals are coming to realize that, far from holding aloof, it is their duty, in the progressive tradition, to ally themselves, through cooperation with the labor movement, with the public whose servants they are.[97]

Union membership itself, because it reduces the powerlessness of individual librarians, has an inhibiting effect on work alienation and burnout. The increased compensation, benefits, and job security that constitute the traditional objectives of collective bargaining help to reduce the extent of worker exploitation, an increasing problem in libraries since the advent of austerity management. Speedups, deskilling, and work fragmentation can be effectively opposed through union negotiation. If library unions are to make a serious assault on the sources of work alienation, however, they must go beyond the bread-and-butter issues and negotiate for workplace democracy. Where management has remained obdurately opposed to genuine employee participation in decision making, the union can be a forceful advocate.

While library union development and union attention to QWL issues can exert a strong restraining influence on work alienation, unions cannot, in themselves, be expected to eliminate the problem. This is because unions, while strengthening the position of workers vis-à-vis management, tacitly accept the basic relationship of management and workers as one of domination and subordination. The very act of collective bargaining, whatever gains are secured for unit members, reinforces and legitimates managerial authority. Sociologist James Rinehart describes unions as paradoxical institutions: "While they are the only effective vehicle workers have a present to advance their interests, they have also become a force for accommodating workers to corporate capitalism."[98] If any union is capable of advancing beyond such an impasse, nevertheless, surely it is one in which the members are not only participants in a professional association committed to the values of work autonomy and public service but also generally the beneficiaries of a humanistically oriented professional education.

Professional education is widely considered to have a significant potential for reducing the incidence and severity of burnout. It is often suggested that the traditional emphasis of professional education—that is, client-centered idealism—promotes unrealistically high expectations among beginning professionals and that the disparity between such expectations and professional realities is a prime factor in the burnout syndrome. Maslach contends that students should be encouraged to develop more "accurate" expectations: "If they did, there would be fewer unpleasant 'surprises' or 'reality shocks' that shatter their ideals or lead them to consider themselves as total failures."[99] For Edelwich and Brodsky, inadequate personal recognition and the subordination of client services to administrative and political requirements are but two of the many "givens" that presumably constitute "the parameters within which all concerned must learn to work."[100]

But should it be the role of professional education to scale down students' expectations? While it is folly, to be sure, to shield students from the realities of professional practice, it would be thoroughly self-defeating systematically to instill attitudes of resignation and accommodation. The idealism, enthusiasm, and even the brash self-confidence that beginning librarians typically bring to their work infuse the profession with new hope and courage. For a profession that has all too often—and with all too much justice—been criticized as passive and reactive, the high expectations of fledgling librarians are a precious resource. Instead of dampening down such idealism in an attempt to reduce future disillusionment, professional education should actively foster idealism, aiding and abetting students in their realization of it. Students should be encouraged to criticize and change the alienating aspects of existing professional practices and paradigms rather than merely to adapt—and they should be armed appropriately.

MLS (Master of Library Science) students should leave library school at least as well equipped to communicate with each other and with library users as with the machinery of their trade. Our current fascination with information technologies must be balanced by careful attention to the more specifically human dimensions of librarianship. The development of the interpersonal skills so essential not only to sensitive and productive interaction with our publics but to our own cooperation in professional problem solving should not be left to informal happenstance. Library students should be introduced to a genuinely representative range of approaches to library management, including the various participative alternatives, and to the ins and outs of labor organization and other political strategies. They should be given a chance to compare notes with the students and practitioners of other professions and, insofar as possible, shown what the research methods and theories of the social sciences can do to help them identify and remove the obstacles to meaningful and rewarding public service that are thrown up by the structural conditions under which contemporary librarianship labors.

Finally, those of us directly engaged in library science research must strive to develop a bit of that "sociological imagination" that, as C. Wright Mills suggests, enables us to distinguish between "personal troubles of milieu" and "public issues of social structure."[101] The value of such a perspective to our ongoing efforts to ascertain and meet the information needs of our clients should be obvious. An awareness of the structural factors involved in the creation and resolution of such problems of our own as burnout and work alienation may well be the sine qua non of our effective survival as a profession.

## NOTES

1. Studs Terkel, *Working* (New York: Pantheon Books, 1972), p. xxiv.

2. Eric Sundstrom, *Work Places: The Psychology of the Physical Environment in Offices and Factories* (Cambridge: Cambridge University Press, 1986), p. 23.

3. Sar A. Levitan and Clifford M. Johnson, *Second Thoughts on Work* (Kalamazoo, Michigan: W. E. Upjohn Institute for Employment Research, 1982), pp. 152–53.

4. Sundstrom, *Work Places,* p. 47.

5. Michael Rose, *Re-Working the Work Ethic: Economic Values and Socio-Cultural Politics* (New York: Schocken Books, 1985), pp. 116–17.

6. Ibid., p. 117.

7. David G. Bowers, "Work Humanization in Practice: What is Business Doing?" in *A Matter of Dignity: Inquiries into the Humanization of Work,* ed. W. J. Heisler and John W. Houck (Notre Dame, Ind.: University of Notre Dame Press, 1977), p. 147.

8. Rose, *Re-Working the Work Ethic,* p. 107.

9. James Rinehart, "Improving the Quality of Working Life Through Job Redesign: Work Humanization or Work Rationalization?" *Canadian Review of Sociology & Anthropology* 23 (November 1986):515.

10. Levitan and Johnson, *Second Thoughts on Work,* p. 163.

11. John Hoerr, "Worker Participation Then and Now," in *Participative Systems at Work: Creating Quality and Employment Security,* ed. Sidney P. Rubinstein (New York: Human Sciences Press, 1987), p. 142.

12. Charles Derber and William Schwartz, "Toward a Theory of Worker Participation," *Sociological Inquiry* 53 (Winter 1983):61.

13. Irving Bluestone, "Work Humanization in Practice: What Can Labor Do?" in *A Matter of Dignity: Inquiries into the Humanization of Work,* ed. W. J. Heisler and John W. Houck, p. 177.

14. "Perot to Smith: GM Must Change," *Newsweek* (December 15, 1986):41.

15. Levitan and Johnson, *Second Thoughts on Work,* p. 164.

16. Rose, *Re-Working the Work Ethic,* p. 111.

17. Rinehart, "Improving the Quality of Working Life Through Job Redesign," p. 518.

18. Ibid., p. 518.

19. Nancy Loving Tubesing and Donald A. Tubesing, "The Treatment of Choice: Selecting Stress Skills to Suit the Individual and the Situation," in *Job Stress and Burnout: Research, Theory, and Intervention Perspectives,* ed. Whiton Stewart Paine (Beverly Hills: Sage Publications, 1982), p. 157.

20. Beverly A. Potter, *Beating Job Burnout* (San Francisco: Harbor Publishing, 1980), p. 29.

21. Annetta Miller, "Stress on the Job," *Newsweek* (April 25, 1988):42.
22. Rebecca Donovan, "Stress in the Workplace: A Framework for Research and Practice," *Social Casework* 68 (May 1987):264.
23. Leonard I. Pearlin and Carmi Schooler, "The Structure of Coping," *Journal of Health and Social Behavior* 19 (March 1978):18.
24. Ayala M. Pines and Elliot Aronson, *Burnout: From Tedium to Personal Growth* (New York: The Free Press, 1981), p. 219.
25. Elizabeth G. Menaghan and Esther S. Merves, "Coping with Occupational Problems: The Limits of Individual Efforts," *Journal of Health and Social Behavior* 25 (December 1984):415.
26. Marybeth Shinn et al., "Coping with Job Stress and Burnout in the Human Services," *Journal of Personality and Social Psychology* 46 (April 1984):874.
27. Donovan, "Stress in the Workplace," p. 264.
28. Pearlin and Schooler, "The Structure of Coping," p. 2.
29. Pines and Aronson, *Burnout;* Shinn et al., "Coping with Job Stress and Burnout in the Human Services"; Marybeth Shinn and Hanne Mørch, "A Tripartite Model of Coping with Burnout," in *Stress and Burnout in the Human Service Professions,* ed. Barry A. Farber (New York: Pergamon Press, 1983); Janina C. Latack, "Coping with Job Stress: Measures and Future Directions for Scale Development," *Journal of Applied Psychology* 71 (August 1986).
30. Donovan, "Stress in the Workplace," p. 262.
31. Richard E. Farmer, Lynn Hunt Monahan, and Reinhold W. Hekeler, *Stress Management for Human Services* (Beverly Hills: Sage Publications, 1984), p. 69.
32. Christina Maslach, *Burnout: The Cost of Caring* (Englewood Cliffs, New Jersey: Prentice-Hall, 1982), p. 102.
33. Jerry Edelwich and Archie Brodsky, *Burnout: Stages of Disillusionment in the Helping Professions* (New York: Human Sciences Press, 1980), p. 212.
34. Maslach, *Burnout: The Cost of Caring,* p. 95; Edelwich and Brodsky, *Burnout: Stages of Disillusionment in the Helping Professions,* pp. 215–17.
35. Pines and Aronson, *Burnout: From Tedium to Personal Growth,* p. 164.
36. Maslach, *Burnout: The Cost of Caring,* p. 91.
37. Pines and Aronson, *Burnout: From Tedium to Personal Growth,* p. 153.
38. Latack, "Coping with Job Stress," no p.
39. Maslach, *Burnout: The Cost of Caring,* p. 101.
40. Ibid., p. 92.
41. Edelwich and Brodsky, *Burnout: Stages of Disillusionment in the Helping Professions,* p. 239.
42. Ayala M. Pines, "On Burnout and the Buffering Effects of Social Support," in *Stress and Burnout in the Human Service Professions,* ed. Barry A. Farber; Shinn et al., "Coping with Job Stress and Burnout in the Human Services"; Joseph F. Constable and Daniel W. Russell, "The Effect of Social Support and the Work Environment Upon Burnout Among Nurses," *Journal of Human Stress* 12 (Spring 1986); David C. Wade, Eric Cooley, and Victor Savicki, "A Longitudinal Study of Burnout," *Children & Youth Services Review* 8 (No. 2, 1986); Sophia Kahill, "Relationship of Burnout Among Professional Psychologists to Professional Expectations and Social Support," *Psychological Reports* 59 (December 1986).
43. Donovan, "Stress in the Workplace," pp. 263–64.
44. Pines, "On Burnout and the Buffering Effects of Social Support," p. 159.

45. Rosemarie Scully, "The Work-Setting Support Group: A Means of Preventing Burnout," in *Stress and Burnout in the Human Service Professions,* ed. Barry A. Farber, pp. 190–91.

46. Maslach, *Burnout: The Cost of Caring,* p. 117.

47. Cary Cherniss, *Professional Burnout in Human Service Organizations* (New York: Praeger, 1980), p. 47.

48. Tubesing and Tubesing, "The Treatment of Choice," in *Job Stress and Burnout,* ed. Whiton Stewart Paine, p. 156.

49. Ayala M. Pines, "Changing Organizations: Is A Work Environment Without Burnout an Impossible Goal?" in *Job Stress and Burnout,* ed. Whiton Stewart Paine, p. 211.

50. Cherniss, *Professional Burnout in Human Service Organizations,* p. 227.

51. Ibid., p. 228.

52. Shinn et al., "Coping with Job Stress and Burnout in the Human Services," p. 874.

53. Cherniss, *Professional Burnout in Human Service Organizations,* p. 230.

54. Maslach, *Burnout: The Cost of Caring,* pp. 127–28.

55. Pines and Aronson, *Burnout: From Tedium to Personal Growth,* pp. 118–19.

56. Mindy Schanbank, "Job Security: A Healthy Bonus," *Psychology Today* 21 (May 1987); Wade, Cooley, and Savicki, "A Longitudinal Study of Burnout."

57. Pines, "Changing Organizations," in *Job Stress and Burnout,* ed. Whiton Stewart Paine, pp. 203–04.

58. Ibid., p. 197.

59. Maslach, *Burnout: The Cost of Caring,* p. 120.

60. Shinn et al., "Coping with Job Stress and Burnout in the Human Services," p. 874.

61. Howard J. Karger, "Burnout as Alienation," *Social Service Review* 55 (June 1981); Ayala M. Pines and Ditsa Kafry, "Occupational Tedium in the Social Services," *Social Work* 23 (November 1978).

62. Pines and Aronson, *Burnout: From Tedium to Personal Growth,* p. 117.

63. Ibid., p. 117.

64. Pines, "Changing Organizations," in *Job Stress and Burnout,* ed. Whiton Stewart Paine, pp. 206–7.

65. Maslach, *Burnout: The Cost of Caring,* p. 146.

66. Ronald M. Mason, *Participatory and Workplace Democracy: A Theoretical Development in Critique of Liberalism* (Carbondale, Illinois: Southern Illinois University Press, 1982), p. 154.

67. Edward S. Greenberg, *Workplace Democracy: The Political Effects of Participation* (Ithaca, New York: Cornell University Press, 1986), pp. 113–14; Mason, *Participatory and Workplace Democracy,* p. 133; Susan E. Jackson, "Participation in Decision Making as a Strategy for Reducing Job-related Strain," *Journal of Applied Psychology* 68 (February 1983).

68. Maurice P. Marchant, "The Effects of the Decision-Making Process and Related Organizational Factors on Alternative Measures of Performance in University Libraries," Ph.D. dissertation, University of Michigan, 1970.

69. Maurice P. Marchant, "Participative Management, Job Satisfaction, and Service," *Library Journal* 107 (April 15, 1982):783.

70. Dale Susan Bengston and Dorothy Shields, "A Test of Marchant's Predictive

Formulas Involving Job Satisfaction," *Journal of Academic Librarianship* 11 (May 1985):92.

71. Nathan M. Smith and Veneese C. Nelson, "Burnout: A Survey of Academic Reference Librarians," *College & Research Libraries* 44 (May 1983):224.

72. Donald J. Sager, *Participatory Management in Libraries* (Metuchen, New Jersey: Scarecrow Press, 1982), p. 49.

73. Mason, *Participatory and Workplace Democracy,* p. 36.

74. Herbert S. White "Participative Management Is the Answer, But What Was the Question?" *Library Journal* 110 (August 1985):63.

75. Sager, *Participatory Management in Libraries,* p. 43.

76. Ibid., p. 47.

77. Deborah A. Mourey and Jerry W. Mansfield, "Quality Circles for Management Decisions: What's In It for Libraries?" *Special Libraries* 75 (April 1984):91; Charles Martell and John Tyson, "Quality Circles," *Journal of Academic Librarianship* 9 (November 1983):286.

78. Sager, *Participatory Management in Libraries,* p. 97.

79. Mourey and Mansfield, "Quality Circles for Management Decisions," p. 92.

80. Jason R. Stone, "Quality Circles in the Library," *New Jersey Libraries* 20 (Summer 1987).

81. James W. Rinehart, *The Tyranny of Work: Alienation and the Labor Process,* 2nd ed. (Toronto: Harcourt, Brace Jovanovich Canada, 1987), p. 183.

82. Terry E. Carrilio and David M. Eisenberg, "Using Peer Support to Prevent Worker Burnout," *Social Casework* 65 (May 1984):310.

83. Derber and Schwartz, "Toward a Theory of Worker Participation," p. 71.

84. Mason, *Participatory and Workplace Democracy,* p. 171.

85. Ibid., p. 171.

86. Ibid., p. 160.

87. Ibid., p. 160.

88. Poul Andersen and Børge Sørenson, "Collective Management in the Public Library: A Study of Collective Management in Denmark with Illustrations from Two Danish Libraries," in *Studies in Library Management,* vol. 7, ed. Anthony Vaughan (London: Clive Bingley, 1982), p. 196.

89. Andersen and Sørenson, "Collective Management in the Public Library," p. 194.

90. Rashelle Schlessinger Karp, "Public Library Unions: Bane or Boon?" in *Advances in Library Administration and Organization,* vol. 4, ed. Gerard B. McCabe and Bernard Kreissman (Greenwich, Connecticut: JAI Press, 1985), p. 25.

91. Theodore Lewis Guyton, *Unionization: The Viewpoint of Librarians* (Chicago: American Library Association, 1975), p. 11.

92. James M. Kusack, *Unions for Academic Library Support Staff: Impact on Workers and the Workplace* (Westport, Connecticut: Greenwood Press, 1986), p. 17.

93. Karp, "Public Library Unions: Bane or Boon?" p. 28.

94. Kusack, *Unions for Academic Library Suppot Staff,* p. 13.

95. Mary Rosenthal, "The Impact of Unions on Salaries in Public Libraries," *Library Quarterly* 55 (January 1985):68; Malcolm Getz, *Public Libraries: An Economic View* (Baltimore: John Hopkins University Press, 1980), p. 71.

96. Bob Carmack and John N. Olsgaard, "Collective Bargaining Among Academic Librarians: A Survey of ACRL Members," *College & Research Libraries* 43 (March 1982):141.

97. William P. Tucker, "Unionization for Special Librarians," *Special Libraries* 30 (February 1939):42–43.

98. Rinehart, *The Tyranny of Work*, p. 194.

99. Maslach, *Burnout: The Cost of Caring*, p. 135.

100. Edelwich and Brodsky, *Burnout: Stages of Disillusionment in the Helping Professions,* p. 129.

101. C. Wright Mills, *The Sociological Imagination* (New York: Oxford University Press, 1959), p. 8.

# Selected Bibliography

Abercrombie, Nicholas; Hill, Stephen; and Turner, Bryan S. *The Dominant Ideology Thesis*. London: George Allen & Unwin, 1980.

Abush, Ronnie, and Burkhead, E. Jane. "Job Stress in Midlife Working Women: Relationships among Personality Type, Job Characteristics, and Job Tension." *Journal of Counseling Psychology* 31 (January 1984):36–44.

Allay, Evelyn. *Working Women's Music: The Songs and Struggles of Women in the Cotton Mills, Textile Plants and Needle Trades*. Somerville, Massachusetts: New England Free Press, 1976.

Andersen, Poul, and Sørenson, Børge. "Collective Management in the Public Library: A Study of Collective Management in Denmark with Illustrations from Two Danish Libraries." In *Studies in Library Management,* Vol. 7, ed. Anthony Vaughan. London: Clive Bingley, 1982.

Anthony, P. D. *The Ideology of Work*. London: Tavistock, 1977.

Arnold, Stephen E. "End-Users: Dreams or Dollars." *Online* 11 (January 1987):71–81.

Atkinson, Hugh C. "Prices of U.S. and Foreign Published Materials." In *The Bowker Annual of Library & Book Trade Information,* 19th ed., ed. Madeline Miele. New York: R. R. Bowker, 1974.

Ballard, Thomas. "Public Library Finance: An Economic Forecast." *Wilson Library Bulletin* 57 (February 1983): 471–74.

Basil, Douglas C., and Cook, Curtis W. *The Management of Change*. Maidenhead, Berkshire, U.K.: McGraw-Hill, 1974.

Baxter, Brian. *Alienation and Authenticity: Some Consequences for Organized Work*. London: Tavistock, 1982.

Bell, Daniel. *The Coming of Post-Industrial Society*. New York: Basic Books, 1973.

Bengston, Dale Susan, and Shields, Dorothy. "A Test of Marchant's Predictive Formulas Involving Job Satisfaction." *Journal of Academic Librarianship* 11 (May 1985):88–92.

Bichteler, Julie. "Human Aspects of High Tech in Special Libraries." *Special Libraries* 77 (Summer 1986):121–28.

Birch, Nancy; Marchant, Maurice P.; and Smith, Nathan M. "Perceived Role Conflict, Role Ambiguity, and Reference Librarian Burnout in Public Libraries." *Library and Information Science Research* 8 (January-March 1986):53–65.

Birdsall, William F. "Librarians and Professionalism: Status Measured by Outmoded Models." *Canadian Library Journal* 37 (June 1980):145–48.

Blake, Fay M. "What's a Nice Librarian Like You Doing Behind a Cash Register?" In *User Fees: A Practical Perspective,* ed. Miriam A. Drake. Littleton, Colorado: Libraries Unlimited, 1981.

Blankenship, Ralph L., ed. *Colleagues in Organization: The Social Construction of Professional Work.* New York: John Wiley & Sons, 1977.

Bluestone, Irving. "Work Humanization in Practice: What Can Labor Do?" In *A Matter of Dignity: Inquiries into the Humanization of Work,* ed. W. J. Heisler and John W. Houck. Notre Dame, Indiana: University of Notre Dame Press, 1977.

Bowers, David G. "Work Humanization in Practice: What Is Business Doing?" In *A Matter of Dignity: Inquiries into the Humanization of Work,* ed. W. J. Heisler and John W. Houck. Notre Dame, Indiana: University of Notre Dame Press, 1977.

Brand, Barbara Elizabeth. "Librarianship and Other Female-Intensive Professions." *Journal of Library History* 18 (Fall 1983):391–406.

Brand, Barbara Elizabeth. "Sex-Typing in Education for Librarianship: 1870–1920." In *The Status of Women in Librarianship: Historical, Sociological, and Economic Issues,* ed. Katherine M. Heim. New York: Neal-Schuman, 1983.

Brod, Craig, and St. John, Wes. *Technostress: The Human Cost of the Computer Revolution.* Reading, Massachusetts: 1984.

Brown, Paul W. "Probation Officer Burnout: An Organizational Disease/An Organizational Cure." *Federal Probation* 50 (March 1986):4–7.

Bucher, Rue, and Stelling, Joan. *Becoming Professional.* Beverly Hills: Sage Publications, 1977.

Budlong, Minnie Clarke. *A Plan of Organization for Small Libraries.* Boston: The Boston Book Company, 1917.

Bundy, Mary Lee. *Challenges to the System.* Urban Information Series Publication No. 2. College Park, Maryland: Urban Information Interpreters, 1972.

Bundy, Mary Lee. *Helping People Take Control: The Public Library's Mission in a Democracy.* College Park, Maryland: Urban Information Interpreters, 1980.

Bundy, Mary Lee, and Wasserman, Paul. "Professionalism Reconsidered." *College and Research Libraries* 29 (January 1968): 5–26.

Caldwell, W. "Libraries and the Social Structure." *Assistant Librarian* 61 (October 1968):214–18.

Calhoun, Daniel C. *Professional Lives in America: Structure and Aspirations, 1750–1850.* Cambridge, Massachusetts: Harvard University Press, 1965.

Carmack, Bob, and Olsgaard, John N. "Collective Bargaining Among Academic Librarians: A Survey of ACRL Members." *College & Research Libraries* 43 (March 1982): 140–45.

Carrilio, Terry E., and Eisenberg, David M. "Using Peer Support to Prevent Worker Burnout." *Social Casework* 65 (May 1984):307–10.

Carroll, Daniel. "Library Marketing: Old and New Truths." *Wilson Library Bulletin* 57 (November 1982): 212–16.

Carroll, Jerome F. X., and White, William L. "Theory Building: Integrating Individual and Environmental Factors Within an Ecological Framework." In *Job Stress and Burnout: Research, Theory, and Intervention Perspectives,* ed. Whiton Stewart Paine. Beverly Hills: Sage Publications, 1982.

Cart, Michael. "Caveats, Qualms, and Quibbles: A Revisionist View of Library Automation." *Library Journal* 112 (February 1, 1987):38–41.

Cedoline, Anthony J. *Job Burnout in Public Education: Symptoms, Causes, and Survival Skills.* New York: Teachers' College Press, 1982.

Cherniss, Cary. *Professional Burnout in Human Service Organizations.* New York: Praeger, 1980.

Cherniss, Cary. *Staff Burnout: Job Stress in the Human Services.* Beverly Hills: Sage Publications, 1980.

Cohen, Marcia B., and Wagner, David. "Social Work Professionalism: Reality and Illusion." In *Professionals as Workers: Mental Labor in Advanced Capitalism,* by Charles Derber. Boston: G. K. Hall, 1982.

Constable, Joseph F., and Russell, Daniel W. "The Effect of Social Support and the Work Environment upon Burnout among Nurses." *Journal of Human Stress* 12 (Spring 1986):20–26.

Crane, Stephen J., and Iwanicki, Edward F. "Perceived Role Conflict, Role Ambiguity, and Burnout among Special Education Teachers." *RASE: Remedial and Special Education* 7 (March-April 1986):24–31.

Dain, Phyllis. *The New York Public Library: A History of Its Founding and Early Years.* New York: New York Public Library, 1972.

Dain, Phyllis. "Women's Studies in American Library History: Some Critical Reflections." *Journal of Library History* 18 (Fall 1983):450–72.

Dakshinamurti, Ganga. "Automation's Effect on Library Personnel." *Canadian Library Journal* 42 (December 1985): 343–51.

"Dallas Public Library Cuts Services and Staff Salaries." *Texas Libraries* 47 (Summer 1986): 55.

Dance, Jim. "Cutback Management: The Detroit Public Library." *Wilson Library Bulletin* 57 (February 1983): 465–70.

D'Elia, George P. "The Determinants of Job Satisfaction among Beginning Librarians." *Library Quarterly* 49 (July 1979): 283–302.

Delmonte, M. M. "Meditation Practice as Related to Occupational Stress, Health, and Productivity." *Perceptual and Motor Skills* 59 (October 1984): 581–82.

"Denver Public Makes Changes to Halt A Long Decline." *Library Journal* 111 (May 15, 1986): 17.

Derber, Charles. *Professionals as Workers: Mental Labor in Advanced Capitalism.* Boston: G. K. Hall, 1982.

Derber, Charles, and Schwartz, William. "Toward a Theory of Worker Participation." *Social Inquiry* 53 (Winter 1983): 61–78.

Deverson, Jane, and Lindsay, Katherine. *Voices From the Middle Class: A Study of Families in Two London Suburbs.* London: Hutchinson, 1975.

Dewey, Melvil. "Women in Libraries: How They Are Handicapped." In *The Role of Women in Librarianship 1876–1976: The Entry, Advancement, and Struggle for Equalization in One Profession,* by Kathleen Weibel and Kathleen M. Heim. Phoenix: Oryx Press, 1979.

Dimock, Marshall E. "The Place of Organization in Institutional Development." In *Current Issues in Library Administration,* ed. Carlton B. Joeckel. Chicago: University of Chicago Press, 1939.

Ditzion, Sidney. *Arsenals of a Democratic Culture: A Social History of the American Public Library Movement in New England and the Middle States from 1850 to 1900.* Chicago: American Library Association, 1947.

Donovan, Rebecca. "Stress in the Workplace: A Framework for Research and Practice." *Social Casework* 68 (May 1987): 259–66.

Dougherty, Richard M. "The Role of Management Consultants in the 1980s." *Library Trends* 28 (Winter 1980): 425–36.

Dougherty, Richard M., and Heinritz, Fred J. *Scientific Management of Library Operations.* New York: Scarecrow Press, 1966.

Dragon, Andrea C. "The Marketing of Public Library Services." *Drexel Library Quarterly* 19 (Spring 1983): 117–32.

DuMont, Rosemary Ruhig. *Reform and Reaction: The Big City Public Library in American Life.* Westport, Connecticut: Greenwood Press, 1977.

Edelwich, Jerry, and Brodsky, Archie. *Burnout: Stages of Disillusionment in the Helping Professions.* New York: Human Sciences Press, 1980.

Ehrenreich, Barbara, and Ehrenreich, John. "Hospital Workers: A Case Study in the 'New Working Class.'" In *Prognosis Negative: Crisis in the Health Care System,* ed. David Kotelchuck. New York: Vintage, 1976.

Etzioni, Amitai, ed. *The Semi-Professions and Their Organization: Teachers, Nurses, Social Workers.* New York: Free Press, 1969.

Fairchild, Salome Cutler. "Women in American Libraries." In *The Role of Women in Librarianship 1876–1976: The Entry, Advancement, and Struggle for Equalization in One Profession,* by Kathleen Weibel and Kathleen M. Heim. Phoenix: Oryx Press, 1979.

Farber, Barry A., ed. *Stress and Burnout in the Human Service Professions.* New York: Pergamon Press, 1983.

Farmer, Richard E.; Monahan, Lynn Hunt; and Hekeler, Reinhold W. *Stress Management for Human Services.* Beverly Hills: Sage Publications, 1984.

"Fat Circ Figures No Fluke, Goldhor Survey Figures Show." *Library Journal* 108 (September 15, 1983): 1750.

Ferriero, David S., and Powers, Kathleen A. "Burnout at the Reference Desk." *RQ* 21 (Spring 1982): 274–79.

Fibkins, William L. "Organizing Helping Settings to Reduce Burnout." In *Stress and Burnout in the Human Service Professions,* ed. Barry A. Farber. New York: Pergamon Press, 1983.

Fiorenza, Francis Schüssler. "Work and Critical Theology." In *A Matter of Dignity: Inquiries into the Humanization of Work,* ed. W. J. Heisler and John W. Houck. Notre Dame, Indiana: University of Notre Dame Press, 1977.

Fischer, Harvey J. "A Psychoanalytic View of Burnout." In *Stress and Burnout in the Human Service Professions,* ed. Barry A. Farber. New York: Pergamon Press, 1983.

Fletcher, William I. *Public Libraries in America.* Boston: Roberts Brothers, 1894.

"Flo Kennedy to Librarians: 'Get Out of Your Rut.'" *American Libraries* 17 (July/August 1986): 547.

Foss, Sam Walter. "The Library and Industrial Workers: Carry the Library to the Workers." *Public Libraries* 13 (March 1908): 82–83.

Foss, Sam Walter. "Man More Than Machinery." *Public Libraries* 12 (April 1907): 117–20.

Frankenhaeuser, Marianne. "Job Demands, Health and Wellbeing." *Reports From the Department of Psychology, University of Stockholm*, No. 517 (December 1977).

Freidson, Eliot. *Professional Powers: A Study of the Institutionalization of Formal Knowledge.* Chicago: University of Chicago Press, 1986.

French, John R. P., Jr., and Caplan, Robert D. "Organizational Stress and Individual Strain." In *The Failure of Success*, ed. Alfred J. Marrow. New York: AMACOM, 1972.

Freudenberger, Herbert J. *Burnout: The High Cost of High Achievement.* New York: Anchor Press, 1980.

Freudenberger, Herbert J. "The Staff Burnout Syndrome in Alternative Institutions." *Psychotherapy: Theory, Research and Practice* 12 (Spring 1975): 73–82.

Fromm, Erich. *Marx's Concept of Man.* New York: Frederick Ungar, 1961.

Fromm, Erich. *The Sane Society.* New York: Rinehart, 1955.

Ganster, Daniel C.; Fusilier, Marcelline R.; and Mayes, Bronston T. "Role of Social Support in the Experience at Work." *Journal of Applied Psychology* 71 (February 1986): 102–10.

Garrison, Dee. *Apostles of Culture: The Public Librarian and Amercian Society, 1876–1920.* New York: The Free Press, 1979.

Geison, Gerald L. *Professions and Professional Ideologies in America.* Chapel Hill: University of North Carolina Press, 1983.

Getz, Malcolm. *Public Libraries: An Economic View.* Baltimore: Johns Hopkins University Press, 1980.

Goode, William. "The Librarian: From Occupation to Profession?" *Library Quarterly* 31 (October 1961): 306–20.

Graf, Francis A. "The Relationship Between Social Support and Occupational Stress Among Police Officers." *Journal of Police Science and Administration* 14 (September 1986): 178–86.

Gray, Carolyn M. "Technology and the Academic Staff or the Resurgence of the Luddites." In *Professional Competencies: Technology and the Librarian*, ed. Linda C. Smith. Urbana-Champaign: Graduate School of Library and Information Science, University of Illinois, 1983.

Greenberg, Edward S. *Workplace Democracy: The Political Effects of Participation.* Ithaca, New York: Cornell University Press, 1986.

Grosser, Kerry. "Burnout Amongst Librarians and Information Workers." *LASIE* 18 (September-October 1987): 32–41.

Grosser, Kerry. "Stress and Stress Management: A Literature Review." *LASIE* 15 (March-April 1985): 2–23.

Guyton, Theodore Lewis. *Unionization: The Viewpoint of Librarians.* Chicago: American Library Association, 1975.

Gwinup, Thomas. "The Failure of Librarians to Attain Profession: the Causes, the Consequences, and the Prospect." *Wilson Library Bulletin* 48 (February 1974): 482–90.

Haack, Mary; Jones, John W.; and Roose, Tina. "Occupational Burnout Among Librarians." *Drexel Library Quarterly* 20 (Spring 1984): 46–72.

Haak, John R. "Goal Determination." In *A Reader in Library Management,* ed. Ross Shimmon. London: Clive Bingley, 1976.

Harris, Michael. "Portrait in Paradox: Commitment and Ambivalence in American Librarianship, 1876–1976." *Libri* 26 (December 1976): 281–301.

Harris, Michael H. *The Purpose of the American Public Library in Historical Perspective: A Revisionist Interpretation.* ERIC Document 071 668. Washington, D.C.: ERIC Clearinghouse on Library and Information Sciences, 1972.

Harris, Michael H. "The Role of the Public Library in American Life: A Speculative Essay." Occasional paper no. 117. Champaign, Illinois: University of Illinois, Graduate School of Library Science, January 1975.

Haug, Marie R., and Sussman, Marvin B. "Professionalism and the Public." *Sociological Inquiry* 39 (Winter 1969): 57–64.

Hawkins, Donald T. "The Commodity Nature of Information." *Online* 11 (January 1987): 67–70.

Heim, Kathleen M., ed. *The Status of Women in Librarianship: Historical, Sociological, and Economic Issues.* New York: Neal-Schuman, 1983.

Heisler, W. J. "Worker Alienation: 1900–1975." In *A Matter of Dignity: Inquiries into the Humanization of Work,* ed. W. J. Heisler and John W. Houck. Notre Dame, Indiana: University of Notre Dame Press, 1977.

Heisler, W. J., and Houck, John W., eds. *A Matter of Dignity: Inquiries into the Humanization of Work.* Notre Dame, Indiana: University of Notre Dame Press, 1977.

Hewins, Carolyn M. "Library Work for Women: Some Practical Suggestions on the Subject." *Library Journal* 16 (September 1891): 273–74.

Hildenbrand, Suzanne. "Ambiguous Authority and Aborted Ambition: Gender, Professionalism, and the Rise and Fall of the Welfare State." *Library Trends* 34 (Fall 1985): 185–98.

Hoerr, John. "Worker Participation Then and Now." In *Participative Systems at Work: Creating Quality and Employment Security,* ed. Sidney P. Rubinstein. New York: Human Sciences Press, 1987.

Illich, Ivan, et al. *Disabling Professions.* London: Marion Boyars, 1977.

Jackson, J. A., ed. *Professions and Professionalization.* Cambridge: Cambridge University Press, 1970.

Jackson, Susan E. "Participation in Decision Making as a Strategy for Reducing Job-Related Strain." *Journal of Applied Psychology* 68 (February 1983): 3–19.

Jones, K. H. "Creative Library Management." In *A Reader in Library Management,* ed. Ross Shimmon. London: Clive Bingley, 1976.

Kahill, Sophia. "Relationship of Burnout among Professional Psychologists to Professional Expectations and Social Support." *Psychological Reports* 59 (December 1986): 1043–51.

Kanungo, Rabindra Nath. *Work Alienation: An Integrative Approach.* New York: Praeger, 1982.

Karger, Howard J. "Burnout as Alienation." *Social Service Review* 55 (June 1981): 270–83.

Keane, Anne; Ducette, Joseph; and Alder, Diane C. "Stress in ICU and Non-ICU Nurses." *Nursing Research* 34 (July-August 1985): 231–36.

Kies, Cosette. *Marketing and Public Relations for Libraries.* Metuchen, New Jersey: Scarecrow Press, 1987.

Kohl, David F. *Administration, Personnel, Buildings and Equipment: A Handbook for Library Management.* Santa Barbara: ABC-Clio Information Services, 1985.

Kotler, Philip. *Marketing for Nonprofit Organizations,* 2nd ed. Englewood Cliffs, New Jersey: Prentice-Hall, 1982.

Kottkamp, Robert B., and Mansfield, John R. "Role Conflict, Role Ambiguity, Powerlessness, and Burnout Among High School Supervisors." *Journal of Research & Development in Education* 18 (Summer 1985): 29-38.

Kusack, James M. *Unions for Academic Library Support Staff: Impact on Workers and the Workplace.* Westport, Connecticut: Greenwood Press, 1986.

Larson, Magali Sarfatti. "Proletarianization and Educated Labor." *Theory and Society* 9 (January 1980): 131–76.

Larson, Magali Sarfatti. *The Rise of Professionalism: A Sociological Analysis.* Berkeley: University of California Press, 1977.

Larue, James. "No Dough: How to Manage When Money is Tight." *Illinois Libraries* 69 (February 1987): 106–12.

Latack, Janina C. "Coping with Job Stress: Measures and Future Directions for Scale Development." *Journal of Applied Psychology* 71 (August 1986): 377–85.

Lauderdale, Michael. *Burnout: Strategies for Personal and Organizational Life: Speculations on Evolving Paradigms.* Austin, Texas: Learning Concepts, 1982.

Law, Herbert E. "The Public Library as a Business Proposition." *Library Journal* 30 (July 1905): 405–8.

Leiter, Michael, and Meechan, Kimberly Ann. "Role Structure and Burnout in the Field of Human Services." *Journal of Applied Behavioral Science* 22 (No. 1, 1986): 47–52.

Lenzini, Rebecca T. "Prices of U.S. and Foreign Published Materials." In *The Bowker Annual of Library and Book Trade Information,* 32nd ed., comp. and ed. Filomena Simora. New York: R. R. Bowker, 1987.

Levine, Murray. "Method of Madness: On the Alienation of the Professional." *Journal of Community Psychology* 10 (January 1982): 3–14.

Levitan, Sar A., and Johnson, Clifford M. *Second Thoughts on Work.* Kalamazoo, Michigan: W. E. Upjohn Institute for Employment Research, 1982.

"Library Funding." *Library Journal* 108 (January 15, 1983): 94–96.

"Low Stress Ranking Rankles Librarians." *American Libraries* 17 (July-August 1986): 502–3.

Lowe, John Adams. *Public Library Administration.* Chicago: American Library Association, 1928.

Lynch, Beverly P. "Libraries as Bureaucracies." *Library Trends* 27 (Winter 1979): 259–67.

Lynn, Laurence E., Jr. *Managing the Public's Business: The Job of the Government Executive.* New York: Basic Books, 1981.

MacFarlane, John. *Library Administration.* London: George Allen, 1898.

Mannheim, E. "Reaction to Alienation." *Kansas Journal of Sociology* 1 (1965): 108–11.

Marchant, Maurice P. "The Effects of the Decision-Making Process and Related Organizational Factors on Alternative Measures of Performance in University Libraries." Ph.D. dissertation, University of Michigan, 1970.

Marchant, Maurice P. "Participative Management, Job Satisfaction, and Service." *Library Journal* 107 (April 15, 1982): 782–84.
Marcuse, Herbert. *One-Dimensional Man: Studies in the Ideology of Advanced Industrial Society.* Boston: Beacon Press, 1964.
Marino, Kenneth E., and White, Sam E. "Departmental Structure, Locus of Control, and Job Stress: The Effect of a Moderator." *Journal of Applied Psychology* 70 (November 1985): 782–84.
Martell, Charles, and Tyson, John. "Quality Circles." *Journal of Academic Librarianship* 9 (November 1983): 285–87.
Marx, Karl. *Capital,* vol. 1. New York: Modern Library, 1906.
Marx, Karl. "Economic and Philosophical Manuscripts." In *Karl Marx: Early Writings,* ed. and tr. T. B. Bottomore. London: C. A. Watts, 1963.
Maslach, Christina. *Burnout: The Cost of Caring.* Englewood Cliffs, New Jersey: Prentice-Hall, 1982.
Maslach, Christina. "Understanding Burnout: Definitional Issues in Analyzing a Complex Phenomenon." In *Job Stress and Burnout: Research, Theory, and Intervention Perspectives,* ed. Whiton Stewart Paine. Beverly Hills: Sage Publications, 1982.
Mason, Ronald M. *Participatory and Workplace Democracy: A Theoretical Development in Critique of Liberalism.* Carbondale, Illinois: Southern Illinois University Press, 1982.
Mathews, Anne J. "The Use of Marketing Principles in Library Planning." In *Marketing for Libraries and Information Agencies,* ed. Darlene E. Weingand. Norwood, New Jersey: Ablex Publishing, 1984.
McCulloch, Arthur, and O'Brien, Larry. "The Organizational Determinants of Worker Burnout." *Children & Youth Services Review* 8 (Spring 1986): 175–90.
McDermott, Diane. "Professional Burnout and its Relation to Job Characteristics, Satisfaction, and Control." *Journal of Human Stress* 10 (Summer 1984): 79–85.
Menaghan, Elizabeth G., and Merves, Esther S. "Coping with Occupational Problems: The Limits of Individual Efforts." *Journal of Health and Social Behavior* 25 (December 1984): 406–23.
Menzies, Heather. *Women and the Chip: Case Studies of the Effects of Informatics on Employment in Canada.* Montreal: The Institute for Research on Public Policy, 1981.
Miller, S. M., and Reissman, Frank. *Social Class and Social Policy.* New York: Basic Books, 1968.
Mills, C. Wright. *The Sociological Imagination.* New York: Oxford University Press, 1959.
Mills, C. Wright. *White Collar: The American Middle Classes.* New York: Oxford University Press, 1951.
Minnehan, Robert F., and Paine, Whiton Stewart. "Bottom Lines: Assessing the Economic and Legal Consequences of Burnout." In *Job Stress and Burnout: Research, Theory, and Intervention Perspectives,* ed. Whiton Stewart Paine. Beverly Hills: Sage Publications, 1982.
Moore, Gale. "Reassessing the Social Impacts of New Technology." *Canadian Library Journal* 44 (December 1987): 420–24.
Moran, Barbara B., and Neenan, Peter A. "The Public Library's Invisible Managers." *Library Journal* 112 (June 15, 1987): 27–29.

Mourey, Deborah A., and Mansfield, Jerry W. "Quality Circles for Management Decisions: What's In It for Libraries?" *Special Libraries* 75 (April 1984): 87–94.

Murphy-Hackett, Ellen S., and Ross, Nancy R. "How One Agency Is Fighting Burnout." *Public Welfare* 42 (Spring 1984): 23–27.

Nauratil, Marcia J. *Public Libraries and Nontraditional Clienteles: The Politics of Special Services.* Westport, Connecticut: Greenwood Press, 1985.

Neff, Walter S. *Work and Human Behavior,* 3rd ed. New York: Aldine, 1985.

Nelson, Bonnie R. "The Chimera of Professionalism." *Library Journal* 105 (October 1, 1980): 2029–33.

Nelson, Veneese C. "Burnout: A Reality for Law Librarians?" *Law Library Journal* 79 (Spring 1987): 267–75.

Newman, Donald. "Vincent Morehouse—He Means Business." *Wilson Library Bulletin* 57 (February 1983): 485–89.

Newton, T. J., and Keenan, A. "Coping with Work-Related Stress." *Human Relations* 38 (February 1985): 107–26.

North, John. "Librarianship: A Profession?" *Canadian Library Journal* 34 (August 1977): 253–57.

Nowack, Mary Jane. "Burnout Syndrome: Its Impact on the Information and Referral Worker." *Information and Referral* 5 (Winter 1983): 33–43.

O'Brien, Nancy Patricia. "The Recruitment of Men into Librarianship, Following World War II." In *The Status of Women in Librarianship: Historical, Sociological, and Economic Issues,* ed. Kathleen M. Heim. New York: Neal-Schuman, 1983.

Oppenheimer, Martin. "The Proletarianization of the Professional." In *Professionalization and Social Change: The Sociological Review Monograph No. 20,* ed. Paul Halmos. Keele, Staffordshire, U.K.: University of Keele, 1973.

Osborne, Larry N. "Satisfaction with Library Systems." In *Advances in Library Administration and Organization: A Research Annual,* vol. 4, ed. Gerard B. McCabe and Bernard Kreissman. Greenwich, Connecticut: JAI Press, 1985.

Paine, Whiton Stewart, ed. *Job Stress and Burnout: Research, Theory, and Intervention Perspectives.* Beverly Hills: Sage Publications, 1982.

Pearlin, Leonard I., and Schooler, Carmi. "The Structure of Coping." *Journal of Health and Social Behavior* 19 (March 1978): 2–21.

Petrie, Keith, and Rotheram, Mary Jane. "Insulators Against Stress: Self-Esteem and Assertiveness." *Psychological Reports* 50 (June, 1982, part 1): 963–66.

Phillips, E. Lakin. *Stress, Health, and Psychological Problems in the Major Professions.* Washington, D.C.: University Press of America, 1982.

Pines, Ayala M. "Changing Organizations: Is a Work Environment Without Burnout an Impossible Goal?" In *Job Stress and Burnout: Research, Theory, and Intervention Perspectives,* ed. Whiton Stewart Paine. Beverly Hills: Sage Publications, 1982.

Pines, Ayala M. "On Burnout and the Buffering Effects of Social Support." In *Stress and Burnout in the Human Service Professions,* ed. Barry A. Farber. New York: Pergamon Press, 1983.

Pines, Ayala M., and Aronson, Elliot. *Burnout: From Tedium to Personal Growth.* New York: Free Press, 1981.

Pines, Ayala M., and Kafry, Ditsa. "Occupational Tedium in the Social Services." *Social Work* 23 (November 1978): 499–507.

Platt, G. Howard. "Public Libraries and Funding Freezes." *Canadian Library Journal* 40 (August 1983): 215–18.

Potter, Beverly A. *Beating Job Burnout.* San Francisco: Harbor Publishing, 1980.

Public Library Association. Goals, Guidelines, and Standards Committee. *The Public Library Mission Statement and Its Imperatives for Service.* Chicago: American Library Association, 1979.

Rawls, James R.; Ullrich, Robert A.; and Nelson, Oscar Tivis, Jr. "A Comparison of Managers Entering or Reentering the Profit and Nonprofit Sectors." *Academy of Management Journal* 18 (September 1975): 616–23.

Reeves, Floyd W. "Some General Principles of Administrative Organization." In *Current Issues in Library Administration,* ed. Carlton B. Joeckel. Chicago: University of Chicago Press, 1939.

Rettig, James. "The Crisis in Academic Reference Work." *Reference Services Review* 12 (Fall 1984): 13–14.

Reynolds, Brian A. "Proactive Management in Public Libraries—in California and in the Nation." In *Advances in Library Administration and Organization: A Research Annual,* vol. 6, ed. Gerard B. McCabe and Bernard Kreissman. Greenwich, Connecticut: JAI Press, 1986.

Reynolds, Dennis. *Library Automation: Issues and Applications.* New York: R. R. Bowker, 1985.

Riggar, T. F. *Stress Burnout: An Annotated Bibliography.* Carbondale, Illinois: Southern Illinois University, 1985.

Rinehart, James. "Improving the Quality of Working Life Through Job Redesign: Work Humanization or Work Rationalization?" *Canadian Review of Sociology and Anthropology* 23 (November 1986): 507–30.

Rinehart, James W. *The Tyranny of Work: Alienation and the Labour Process,* 2nd ed. Toronto: Harcourt, Brace Jovanovich Canada, 1987.

Robbins, Jane. *Citizen Participation and Public Library Policy.* Metuchen, New Jersey: Scarecrow Press, 1975.

Rochell, Carlton. *Dreams Betrayed: Working in the Technological Age.* Lexington, Massachusetts: Lexington Books, 1987.

Romaine, Harry. "The Censor." *Library Journal* 16 (June 1891): 168.

Rose, Michael. *Re-Working the Work Ethic: Economic Values and Socio-Cultural Politics.* New York: Schocken Books, 1985.

Rosenblum, Joseph. "Technocrats and Mandarins: The Two Cultures of Librarianship." *The Southeastern Librarian* 31 (Summer 1981): 68–70.

Rosenthal, Mary. "The Impact of Unions on Salaries in Public Libraries." *Library Quarterly* 55 (January 1985): 52–70.

Rouse, William B., and Morris, Nancy M. "Understanding and Enhancing User Acceptance of Computer Technology." *IEEE Transactions on Systems, Man, & Cybernetics* 16 (November-December 1986): 965–73.

Rubin, Lillian Breslow. *Worlds of Pain: Life in the Working-Class Family.* New York: Basic Books, 1976.

Rubinstein, Sidney P., ed. *Participative Systems at Work: Creating Quality and Employment Security.* New York: Human Services Press, 1987.

Ryan, William. *Blaming the Victim.* New York: Random House, 1976.

Sager, Donald J. *Participatory Management in Libraries.* Metuchen, New Jersey: Scarecrow Press, 1982.

Sakharov, Mae, and Farber, Barry A. "A Critical Study of Burnout in Teachers." In *Stress and Burnout in the Human Service Professions,* ed. Barry A. Farber. New York: Pergamon Press, 1983.

Savicki, Victor, and Cooley, Eric. "The Relationship of Work Environment and Client Contact to Burnout in Mental Health Professionals." *Journal of Counseling & Development* 65 (January 1987): 249–52.

Scheppke, James. "The Case Against Marketing." *Texas Libraries* 44 (July 1983): 85–87.

Schwartz, Gail Garfield, and Neikirk, William. *The Work Revolution.* New York: Rawson Associates, 1983.

Scully, Rosemarie. "The Work-Setting Support Group: A Means of Preventing Burnout." In *Stress and Burnout in the Human Service Professions,* ed. Barry A. Farber. New York: Pergamon Press, 1983.

Selye, Hans. *The Stress of Life.* New York: McGraw-Hill, 1976.

Sexton, William P. "Work Humanization in Practice: What Should Business Do?" In *A Matter of Dignity: Inquiries into the Humanization of Work,* ed. W. J. Heisler and John W. Houck. Notre Dame, Indiana: Notre Dame University Press, 1977.

Shaffer, Dale E. *The Maturity of Librarianship as a Profession.* Metuchen, New Jersey: Scarecrow Press, 1968.

Shaughnessy, Thomas W. "Theory Building in Librarianship." *Journal of Library History* 11 (April 1976): 167–76.

Shaw, Dale G.; Keiper, Robert W.; and Flaherty, Charles E. "Stress Causing Events for Teachers." *Education* 106 (Fall 1985): 72–77.

Shaw, Deborah, ed. *Human Aspects of Library Automation: Helping Staff and Patrons Cope.* Urbana-Campaign: Graduate School of Library and Information Science, 1986.

Shimmon, Ross, ed. *A Reader in Library Management.* London: Clive Bingley, 1976.

Shinn, Marybeth, and Mørch, Hanne. "A Tripartite Model of Coping with Burnout." In *Stress and Burnout in the Human Service Professions,* ed. Barry A. Farber. New York: Pergamon Press, 1983.

Shinn, Marybeth; Rosario, Margaret; Mørch, Hanne; and Chestnut, Dennis E. "Coping with Job Stress and Burnout in the Human Services." *Journal of Personality and Social Psychology* 46 (April 1984): 864–76.

Shorter, Edward. "The History of Work in the West: An Overview." In *Work and Community in the West,* ed. Edward Shorter. New York: Harper and Row, 1973.

Simpson, Richard L., and Simpson, Ida Harper. "Women and Bureaucracy in the Semi-Professions." In *The Semi-Professions and Their Organization: Teachers, Nurses, Social Workers,* ed. Amitai Etzioni. New York: Free Press, 1969.

Smith, Nathan M.; Birch, Nancy E.; and Marchant, Maurice P. "Stress, Distress, and Burnout: A Survey of Public Reference Librarians." *Public Libraries* 23 (Fall 1984): 83–85.

Smith, Nathan M., and Nelson, Veneese C. "Burnout: A Survey of Academic Reference Librarians." *College & Research Libraries* 44 (May 1983): 245–50.

Smith, Nathan M., and Nielson, Laura F. "Burnout: A Survey of Corporate Librarians." *Special Libraries* 75 (July 1984): 221–27.

"Statement on Professional Ethics, 1975." *American Libraries* 6 (April 1975): 231.

Stone, Jason R. "Quality Circles in the Library." *New Jersey Libraries* 20 (Summer 1987): 13–19.

Storey, R. A. "Prospect and Prejudice, or Women and Librarianship 1880–1914; A Fourth Footnote." *Library History* 7 (No. 1, 1985): 21–22.

Sundstrom, Eric. *Work Places: The Psychology of the Physical Environment in Offices and Factories.* Cambridge: Cambridge University Press, 1986.

Sze, William C., and Ivker, Barry, "Stress in Social Workers: The Impact of Setting and Role." *Social Casework* 67 (March 1986): 141–48.

Taylor, Frederick Winslow. *The Principles of Scientific Management.* New York: Harper and Brothers, 1919.

Terkel, Studs. *Working: People Talk About What They Do All Day and How They Feel About What They Do.* New York: Pantheon Books, 1972.

Thackeray, R. J. "Boredom and Monotony as a Consequence of Automation: A Consideration of the Evidence Relating Boredom and Monotony Stress." *FAA Office of Aviation Medicine Reports* (February 1980, No. 80-81).

Tubesing, Nancy Loving, and Tubesing, Donald A. "The Treatment of Choice: Selecting Stress Skills to Suit the Individual and the Situation." In *Job Stress and Burnout: Research, Theory, and Intervention Perspectives,* ed. Whiton Stewart Paine. Beverly Hills: Sage Publications, 1982.

Tucker, William P. "Unionization for Special Librarians." *Special Libraries* 30 (February 1939): 41–45.

Turner, J. "Computers in Bank Clerical Functions: Implications for Productivity and the Quality of Working Life." Ph.D. dissertation, Columbia University, 1980.

U.S. Department of Commerce, Bureau of the Census. *Statistical Abstract of the United States, 1987.* 107th ed. Washington, D.C.: U.S. Government Printing Office, 1986.

Usherwood, Bob. "Management and the Meaning of Work." In *Studies in Library Management,* vol. 7, ed. Anthony Vaughan. London: Clive Bingley, 1982.

Usherwood, R. C. "Professional Values in a Bureaucratic Structure." *Library Review* 29 (Spring 1980): 8–14.

Van House, Nancy A. *Public Library User Fees: The Use and Finance of Public Libraries.* Westport, Connecticut: Greenwood Press, 1983.

Vann, Sarah K., ed. *Melvil Dewey: His Enduring Presence in Librarianship.* Littleton, Colorado: Libraries Unlimited, 1978.

Van Orsdol, Mary. "Burnout and Rejuvenation." *Unabashed Librarian* (1986, No. 61): 20.

Wade, David C.; Cooley, Eric; and Savicki, Victor. "A Longitudinal Study of Burnout." *Children & Youth Services Review* 8 (1986, No. 2): 161–73.

Walliman, Isidor. *Estrangement: Marx's Conception of Human Nature and the Division of Labor.* Westport, Connecticut: Greenwood Press, 1981.

Wasserman, Paul. *The New Librarianship: A Challenge for Change.* New York: R. R. Bowker, 1972.

Watts, E. Spencer, and Samuels, Alan R. "What Business Are We In? Perceptions of the Roles and Purposes of the Public Library as Reflected in Professional Literature." *Public Libraries* 23 (Winter 1984): 130–34.

Weber, Max. *From Max Weber: Essays in Sociology,* ed. Hans H. Gerth and C. Wright Mills. London: Routledge & Kegan Paul, 1948.

Weibel, Kathleen, and Heim, Kathleen M. *The Role of Women in Librarianship 1876-1976: The Entry, Advancement, and Struggle for Equalization in One Profession.* Phoenix: Oryx Press, 1979.

Weingand, Darlene E., ed. *Marketing for Libraries and Information Agencies.* Norwood, New Jersey: Ablex Publishing, 1984.

W. E. Upjohn Institute for Employment Research. *Work in America: Report of a Special Task Force to the Secretary of Health, Education, and Welfare.* Cambridge, Massachusetts: MIT Press, 1973.

Wharton, Amy, and Burris, Val. "Office Automation and Its Impact on Women Workers." *Humboldt Journal of Social Relations* 10 (Spring-Summer 1983): 112–26.

White, Herbert S. "Participative Management Is the Answer, but What Was the Question?" *Library Journal* 110 (August 1985): 62–63.

White, Lawrence J. *The Public Library in the 1980s: The Problems of Choice.* Lexington, Massachusetts: Lexington Books, 1983.

Wilder, Jack F., and Plutchick, Robert. "Preparing the Professional: Building Prevention into Training." In *Job Stress and Burnout: Research, Theory, and Intervention Perspectives,* ed. Whiton Stewart Paine. Beverly Hills: Sage Publications, 1982.

Williamson, Charles C. *Training for Library Service: A Report Prepared for the Carnegie Corporation of New York.* Boston: Merrymount Press, 1923.

Williamson, William Landram. *William Frederick Poole and the Modern Library Movement.* New York: Columbia University Press, 1963.

Winter, Michael F. "The Professionalization of Librarianship." Occasional Paper No. 160. Champaign, Illinois: University of Illinois, Graduate School of Library and Information Science, July 1983.

Zastrow, Charles. "Understanding and Preventing Burnout." *British Journal of Social Work* 14 (April 1984): 141–45.

Zweizig, Douglas L. "Lifelong Learning and the Library: The Public Library Response to *A Nation at Risk.*" *Public Libraries* 23 (Fall 1984): 70–75.

# Index

Affirmative action, 91
AFL-CIO, 102
ALA (American Library Association), 42, 43, 45, 51, 52, 56
Alienation, 8; automation and, 72; burnout and, 87; Hegel on, 15; labor and, 13; managers and, 75; Marx on, 15-18 25, 72; privatization of information and, 78; sex segregation in librarianship and, 50-51; social structure and, 105; tactics for elimination of, 90-91, 92, 101; unions and, 25
American Federation of State, County, and Municipal Employees (AFSCME), 102
Amherst College, views on women as librarians, 47
Anarchism, 39
Andersen, Poul, 101
Architects, professional association of, 20
Aristotle, 12, 98
Aronson, Elliot, 2, 30, 88, 90, 95
AT&T, 75, 78, 85, 86
Austerity management. *See* Management styles
Authoritarianism, 40, 41, 51
Automation, 68, 69, 70; capital intensity of, 71; computer-based service, demand for, 64; effects on staff and, 70, 71, 72, 73, 91

Ballard, Thomas, 65
Barash, Theodore, 87
Baumol, William J., 64
Bell, Daniel, 21
Biofeedback, 89. *See also* Stress
Birdsall, William, 52, 53
Bluestone, Irving, 85
Bowers, David, 84
Brand, Barbara, 48
Brigham Young University, study of librarian job satisfaction, 97
British Museum, on women librarians, 48
Brod, Craig, 72, 73
Brodsky, Archie, 89, 91, 104
Bundy, Mary Lee, 53
Burnout, 2, 32, 37, 54, 88; capitalist society and, 101; causes of, 83; effects of, 3, 28, 87, 92; professions other than librarianship and, 4, 5, 6, 7; solutions to, 7, 92, 100, 101-2, 105; symptoms of, 29, 30. *See also* Alienation
*A Burntout Case*, 2

Calvinism, 12, 13
Caplan, Robert D., 30, 31

# Index

Carlyle, Thomas, 13
Carnegie, Andrew, 39
Cart, Michael, 69
"The Censor," 40
Censorship, 56
Cherniss, Cary, 2, 4, 28, 30, 92, 93
Chicago Public Library, 39, 98
Collective bargaining, 102, 103
Commodity, information as, 76
Computer. *See* Automation
Computerization. *See* Automation
Consultative management. *See* Management styles
Coping strategies. *See* Stress
Cutbacks. *See* Funding
Cutter, Charles A., 38

Dain, Phyllis, 50
*Decameron*, bowdlerized editions of, 40
Decision-making, 96, 97
Demotions (Denver Public Library), 68
Derber, Charles, 100
Deskilling, 25, 54, 71, 73, 91, 95, 103
Dewey, Melvil, 42, 44, 48, 49, 51, 68
Dougherty, Richard M., 67
Dragon, Andrea, 76, 78
*Dreams Betrayed*, understanding work in, 70–71
Duluth Public Library (Minn.), QC (quality circle) establishment and, 99
DuMont, Rosemary Ruhig, 40

East Brunswick Public Library (N.J), QC (quality circle) establishment and, 99
Edelwich, Jerry, 89, 91, 104
Elitism, early libraries and, 40-41
Etzioni, Amitai, 26
Everett, Edward, 38

Fairchild, Salome Cutler, 48
Faulkner, William, 11
Fine, Sara, 71, 72
Fischer, Harvey J., 28
Fletcher, William I., 47
Folsom, Charles, 46
Forbes Burnout Survey, 5
Ford, Henry, 14, 15
French, John R. P., 30, 31

French Revolution, 20
Freudenberger, Herbert, 2, 28
Fromm, Erich, 15, 17
Fugs, The, 83n
Funding for libraries, 63; budget cutbacks, 64
Fund-raising, 65

Garrison, Dee, 38, 39, 44, 50, 51
General Motors, 85
George Harris (in *Uncle Tom's Cabin*), 1, 2
Getz, Malcolm, 66
Goal displacement, 57
Goode, William, 51, 52, 55
Gray, Carolyn M., 70
Green, Samual Swet, 76
Greene, Graham, 2

Harris, Michael, 38, 55
Hawthorne Effect, 84, 93
Haug, Marie R., 53
Hegel, G. W. F., 15
Heinritz, Fred J., 67
Hewins, Carolyn, 43
Hodgson, James, 74
Hollerith, Herman, 69
Huntington Beach Library (Calif.), streamlined operations in, 68

IBM, data processors by, 69
Illich, Ivan, 21
Industrialization, 14

Job satisfaction, 97
Job security, 94
Johnson, Walter, 75n

Karger, Howard, 29
Kies, Cossette, 76, 77, 78
Kotler, Philip, 76, 77, 78

Lawyers, professional association of, 20
Levine, Murray, 43
Levitan, Sar A., 86
Librarians: academic, 23; children's, 47, 51; corporate, 31, 97; professional association of, 20; reference, 5, 6

Librarianship, academic, 49; feminization of, 49, 50, 51; masculinization of, 49
Library, public, role of, 56-57
Library education, 51, 101
*Library Journal*, 40, 76
*Library Notes*, 42
Library promotion, marketing, 76, 77, 78
Library Services Act, 64
Library Services and Construction Act (LSCA), 64
Library unions, 101. *See also* Unionization
Library users: funding and, 94; guaging quality of service to, 95; librarians' opinions of, 92
Lincoln Library (Springfield, Ill.), 65
Los Angeles Public Library, fund-raising and, 65
Luther, Martin, 12
Lynn, Laurence E., Jr., 66, 67

MacFarlane, John, 48
*Madame Bovary*, banning of, 40. *See also* Censorship
Management consultants, 73, 74
Management styles: austerity, 65, 68, 94, 95; autocratic, 75; consultative, 97; human relations, 67, 84; participative, 85, 91, 96, 97, 98, 100, 101; scientific, 14, 44, 45, 46, 67; workplace democracy and, 96-97, 100, 101
Marchant, Maurice P., 97
Marcuse, Herbert, 17, 18
Marketing. *See* Library promotion
*Marketing for Nonprofit Organizations*, 76
*Marketing and Public Relations for Libraries*, 76
Marx, Karl, 15, 16, 17, 30, 72
Marxist views on alienation, 18, 25, 57. *See also* Alienation
Maslach, Christina, 2, 5, 6, 7, 27, 28, 30, 89, 90, 92, 93, 95, 96, 104
Maslach Burnout Inventory (MBI), 5
Mason, Ronald, 96-97
Mechanization, 22. *See also* Automation

Mercer County Public Library (Harrodsburg, Ky.), fund-raising and, 65
Metro Toronto Reference Library, reorganization of, 24
Mills, C. Wright, 23, 104
Minnehan, Robert, 4
Moore, Gale, 70
Morehouse, Vincent, 75

*Nation at Risk, A*, 56
National Institute of Mental Health, 99
National Library Week, 76
Nelson, Bonnie, 52, 53
Nelson, Vaneese, 7
New York City, library cutbacks in, 64. *See also* Funding
New York Public Library (NYPL), patron control and, 40; first public library union, 102
New York State Library School (Albany), 43
Nonprofit organizations, marketing of, 76
Nurses, 7, 26, 31, 90

OCLC (Ohio College Library Center), 69

Paine, Whiton Stewart, 4
Parsons, Talcott, 21
Participative management. *See* Management styles
*Participatory Management in Libraries*, 98
Perot, H. Ross, 85
Physicians, professional association of, 20
Pines, Ayala M., 2, 6, 27, 30, 88, 90, 92, 95
Police in libraries, 40
Poole, William Frederick, 38, 39, 42, 47
Potter, Beverly, 87
Prentice, Ann E., 63, 65
*Principles of Scientific Management*, 44
Professional autonomy, 50, 51, 53-54, 57, 67, 68, 91, 93, 96
Professional identity, 20, 43
Professional status, 52

Professionalism, 51, 53; discouragement of, 55
Professionalization, 52
Profit-making techniques, 43, 66
Profit motive. *See* Profit-making techniques
Proletarianization, 22, 26, 30, 32, 55, 71. *See also* Deskilling
Proposition 13 (Calif.), 64
Proposition 2½ (Mass.), 64
*Protestant Ethic and the Spirit of Capitalism, The*, 13
*Public Libraries*, 42
Public Library Inquiry, 64

Quality circles (QCs), 85, 98, 99, 101. *See also* Management styles
Quality of worklife (QWL) movement, 84, 85, 86, 87, 103. *See also* Working conditions

Rawson, H., 47
*Readers' Guide*, 90
Reynolds, Brian A., 68
Reynolds, Dennis, 69, 70
Rinehart, James, 31, 86, 103
Rochell, Carlton, 71
Rose, Michael, 86
Rubin, Lillian, 19

Sager, Donald, 68, 98
St. Benedict, 12
Salaries, 47, 48
San Francisco, 1
Schwartz, William, 100
*Scientific Management of Library Operations*, 67
Sex segregation, among librarians, 49
Sexism, 50
Silas Bronson Library (Waterbury, Conn.), 39
Simpson, Ida Harper, 51, 55
Simpson, Richard L., 51, 55
Smith, Lloyd Pearsall, 39
Smith, Nathan, 5
Social workers, 7, 26; professional association of, 20
Socialism, 39

Sorensen, Borge, 101
Staff Burnout Scale for Health Professionals (SBS), 6
Stowe, Harriet Beecher, 1
Stress, 1, 7, 27, 30; causes of, 96; coping and management of, 32, 87, 88, 89, 90, 93; job strain and, 2; psychosomatic symptoms and, 90. *See also* Burnout
Sussman, Marvin B., 53

Taylor, Frederick Winslow, 14, 15, 44
Taylorism, 45, 84
Teachers, 7, 26; professional association of, 20
Terkel, Studs, 83
Thoreau, Henry David, on employment, 13n
Ticknor, George, 38
Toronto, Metro Reference Library. *See* Metro Toronto Reference Library
Tubesing, Donald, 87
Tubesing, Nancy, 87
Tucker, William P., 103

*Uncle Tom's Cabin*, 1, 2
Unionization, 102, 103
United Auto Workers, 85
University of Texas library, 69
User fees, 67; library admission charges, 75

Van House, Nancy A., 67

Waldenbooks, profit and, 65
Weber, Max, 13
Weberian bureaucratic ideal, 23
Western Electric Company, 84
*White Collar*, 23
White, Herbert S., 46, 98
White, Lawrence J., 56, 66, 67
Williamson Report (Charles C. Williamson), 51
Winsor, Justin, 40, 47
Winter, Michael, 52
Work, 11; ancient Greeks and, 11, 12; ancient Jews and, 12; ancient Romans and, 11; Carlyle, Thomas on, 13; in

Reformation, 12; Thoreau, Henry David on, 13n
Work environment, quality of, 54, 94, 95. *See also* Work reform; Working conditions
Work reform, 86
Worker autonomy, 99, 100. *See also* Professional autonomy

Working conditions, 83; improvement of, 94, 96
Workmen's Compensation Acts, 83
Workplace democratization, 98. *See also* Management styles

Zastrow, Charles, 28
Zweizig, Douglas, 56

**About the Author**

MARCIA J. NAURATIL was a library consultant and taught courses in library and information science at the University of Toronto.

Nauratil, Marcia J.
Z
682.35  The alienated
P82     librarian
N38
1989

| DATE DUE | | | |
|---|---|---|---|
| | | | |
| | | | |
| | | | |
| | | | |
| | | | |
| | | | |
| | | | |
| | | | |
| | | | |
| | | | |

AUDREY COHEN COLLEGE LIBRARY
75 Varick St. 12th Floor
New York, NY 10013